Tadao Yamaguchi

Light on the Origins of Reiki

A Handbook for Practicing the Original Reiki of Usui and Hayashi

Foreword by Frank Arjava Petter

Translated by Ikuko Hirota

T0164050

LOTUS PRESS
SHANGRI-LA

First English Edition 2007
© by Lotus Press
Box 325, Twin Lakes, WI 53181, USA
web: www.lotuspress.com
e-mail: lotuspress@lotuspress.com
The Shangri-La Series is published in cooperation
with Schneelöwe Verlagsberatung, Federal Republic of Germany
© 2006 by Windpferd Verlagsgesellschaft mbH, Aitrang, Germany
All rights reserved
Translated by Ikuko Hirota
Edited by Neehar Douglass
Editor and publisher thank Frank Arjava Petter for professional
advise and his kind support
Cover design by Peter Krafft, Designagentur, Bad Krozingen,
Germany
Layout: Marx Grafik & ArtWork
Pictures: on pages 26, 28, 30, 32, 35, 39, 42, 44, 46, 60, 68, 70, 145, 148,
154 © Tadao Yamaguchi, on pages 62, 101, 102, 109 © Ikuko Hirota,
on page 106 I.H.M Inc.
ISBN: 978-0-9149-5565-8
Library of Congress Control Number 2007920816
Printed in the United States of America

Table of Contents

Foreword

It is my great pleasure and honor to introduce Tadao Yamaguchi's second book.

In 1996 I found myself in a similar situation to Tadao. In those days there was little information available about the origins of Reiki and through a series of 'coincidences' I was discovered by my friend Walter Lübeck. He passed the relay baton to me and today, with pleasure, I pass it on to Tadao Yamaguchi. I don't know anyone who would be more capable of describing the roots of Reiki than Tadao.

Jikiden Reiki, the way it was taught by Hayashi Sensei, convinces by its refreshingly simple clarity. The teaching is not tainted by Western thought and concentrates on the essential.

When Tadao and his mother Chiyoko appeared in the Japanese Reiki sky at the end of the 90's they were not aware of what they actually held in their hands. Tadao grew up with Reiki and had already received Reiki in his mother's belly. Meanwhile more than 50 years have passed and I am not aware of anyone who has the same wealth of Reiki experience and, most importantly, who is also willing and able to share his knowledge with others.

In a conversation Tadao once told me that he compares the energy of his mother with the energy of fire. It rises up, concentrates totally on the practical aspect of the work and in this way burns the non-essential. His own energy Tadao compares with that of water. It flows in all directions and is distributed to the thirsty. When those two energies meet and unite an energy field is created that covers all levels. And in this way they conquer your heart.

Frank Arjava Petter

Prologue: Reiki Meets 靈氣

Reiki—the great art of healing with the hands was originated in Japan and is now practiced by millions of people around the world. It was founded by the great man Mikao Usui Sensei[1] and became popular throughout the West through the contributions of Chujiro Hayashi Sensei and his student, Mrs. Hawayo Takata. However it seems to have at one time disappeared in its homeland—Japan. Now the Reiki, which is practiced in Japan, is mostly the reintroduced form from the West, so some people call it 'Western' Reiki.

Leaders of Western Reiki have tried to track down the roots of Reiki in Japan but have found little information. Failing to find people who had been directly initiated by Usui Sensei or Hayashi Sensei they concluded that it would be impossible to learn the original styles of Reiki there.

However there are still some people in Japan who have preserved the traditional teachings. In fact my mother was one of them. I grew up in good health thanks to my mother's Reiki. She treated me whenever I hurt myself or fell ill, especially when I was a little boy. All my relatives practice Reiki. Some of them, including my mother, have been qualified as a *Shihan* (teacher) who can initiate others. When I was younger I thought Reiki was some kind of traditional secret art kept within my family. I had no idea that it had become so prevalent in the world or that people were searching for the information we had.

Before I started teaching Reiki I was engaged in my family business. Alongside that I was involved in promoting various activities regarding environmental issues and I always had the idea of setting up an NGO in this field. I often attended meetings on environmental issues where I had the chance to meet a lot of people from different fields. It was there that I had my first encounter with other Reiki people. I sometimes exchanged business cards with the participants at those meetings and I picked up a few cards entitled 'Reiki Teacher'. I started to wonder:

"Why is 'Reiki' written in *Katakana* letters (Japanese phonetic letters used to describe foreign words) suggesting that it is a foreign thing?" One day I decided to ask a question of someone whose business card said 'Reiki Teacher'. I asked him why it was not written in the original *Kanji* characters (Japanese writing system coming from Chinese[2]). He answered, "There are no longer any traditional Japanese Reiki practitioners in Japan. If you want to learn Reiki the only way to do it is to learn the Reiki which has been reintroduced from the West." I told him that my mother had learned Reiki directly from Hayashi Sensei over 60 years before (in 1938). That was a great surprise to this Reiki teacher. He rushed back to Tokyo to tell his own teacher the news. His teacher is very famous in the Reiki community in Japan and the news surprised him so greatly that he promptly came all the way to Kyoto to meet my mother. Later he reported the conversation he had with my mother in his book. The impact of the reference in the book was so enormous that a lot of well-known Reiki teachers visited my mother and tried to persuade us to start teaching the original form of Reiki that she had learned from Hayashi Sensei. This was the very first cue for us to set up the **Jikiden Reiki Kenkyukai** (institute) and to start seminars (1999).

Of course the most important motivation for me in starting *Jikiden Reiki* seminars was my desire to pass on what my mother had learned from Hayashi Sensei as accurately as possible. Moreover, by introducing my mother's experience, I wanted to make people understand that Reiki is very effective as a great alternative to modern medicine. Throughout her life my mother healed a lot of people of a wide range of illnesses.

The founder, Usui Sensei, had initially intended to develop Reiki to cure physical illnesses. A lot of Reiki schools today focus only on spiritual development and don't take the healing of physical illness seriously. However I believe that the main purpose of Reiki should be the healing of diseases. If the primary reason for you to receive or learn Reiki is only for your own healing, it is totally relevant. Diseases often guide us to awareness of the unknown. The experience of becoming ill and recovering is very meaningful because it gives us an opportunity to grow through the healing experience. Our direct teacher Hayashi Sensei also taught Reiki as a means of curing physical problems. So I conduct seminars focusing on healing physical illness.

I also hear that the Reiki, which is spread today, is treated as a means of 'relaxation' or 'consolation'. This is of course a part of its effectiveness but I would like to emphasize the immeasurable possibilities it has in more practical applications. In the past Usui Sensei and Hayashi Sensei promoted Reiki in the hope of applying it in medical treatments. Respecting their intention, I am going to continue promoting Reiki as a great way to improve health. I would like to introduce it to as large number of medical professionals as possible and reintroduce the original Reiki to those who have learned the Western form so as to demonstrate its practical uses.

When Western Reiki teachers in Japan visited us one after the other several years ago we were very surprised to learn that some of them had become teachers without any experience of giving treatment. I wondered what Reiki could be without doing treatments. Whenever we had a teacher in our house my mother would always ask them what illnesses they had dealt with in the past. She did not mean to be rude or critical but was just curious because she had assumed that they had had an abundance of treatment experience and wanted to exchange opinions. When she asked this question their faces would go blank and they would answer, without hesitation, that they had never done any treatments at all. I am not saying all Reiki teachers are like this. I think perhaps some schools give the Reiki Teacher qualification too easily. We were quite disappointed in the situation in those days.

However one day we had a visit from a couple of Reiki masters from Europe who were very happy to talk with my mother about their great treatment experiences. They had dealt with a variety of serious diseases like cancer and AIDS. I remember them complaining that people would come to them only after their diseases had become very serious and it would take a very long time to treat them. They wished their clients would decide to come much sooner. I totally understood what they meant because we had also encountered such situations. A lot of the people came to us to receive Reiki after their doctors had given up on them. It was like a 'last straw' for them. Reiki can help, even in these kinds of serious situations, but such treatments require lot of time and patience. Anyway, meeting these masters from Europe brought us a happy surprise and it made us understand why Reiki had spread so widely in the Western countries. Also I hear of some practitioners in the West who use Reiki quite practically in hospitals and have had great results. This makes me believe that a bright future lies before us. I greatly respect what these teachers are doing in the West.

In Japan today modern medicine is so prevalent that we are slow in adapting to alternative medicine (which used to be our 'mainstream' medicine), but I am sure there will be a positive change here too. I think we Japanese can learn a lot from what people on the other side of the globe are doing to facilitate change.

I had this book published in Japanese in 2003 in the hope of causing Japanese people to change their minds. Now I am happy to have it translated into other languages. When I wrote it for Japanese readers I did not imagine that it would be published for non-Japanese people. In order to meet the interests of non-Japanese readers I have rearranged some parts and written additional manuscripts. I hope this book will guide you to a further understanding of Reiki.

January 2007, Tadao Yamaguchi, *Jikiden Reiki Kenkyukai*

Chapter 1:

Some Words about Jikiden Reiki

LINEAGES OF REIKI — FROM JAPAN TO THE WEST

Reiki has become known worldwide today due to the contribution of a lady named Mrs. Hawayo Takata (1900-1980). She brought Reiki to the West and it gradually spread to people all around the globe.

Mrs. Takata was a second generation Japanese American born in Hawaii. In 1935, just before World War II broke out, she was sent to her mother country, Japan, for medical treatment for an illness that had affected her heart, stomach, lungs and gallbladder. Her husband had already passed away and she felt that time was running out. In case the worst should happen she wanted to be prepared by leaving her small daughters in the care of her Japanese parents.

Her condition became worse and worse during her stay in Japan so she had no option but to undergo a serious operation. However just as she lay down on the operating table she heard an internal voice say: "This operation is not necessary." The voice repeated the message three times and it had such an impact on her that she decided to stop the operation. The nurse was very surprised to hear this but made an effort to understand her.

When she asked the doctor if there was not any other way to save her life he replied with kindness, sincerely telling her that there was, but it would take a long time to recover. He introduced her to Hayashi Sensei and Reiki that was to save her life.

Whether by Universal Intention or by a miracle she had been led to Reiki and Hayashi Sensei. After eight months of treatment she had made a miraculous recovery. Hayashi Sensei conducted a Reiki center in Shinano-cho, which in those days was in central Tokyo. The center was quite big enough to accommodate eight Reiki tables and sixteen practitioners, and it was here that Mrs. Takata was a patient.

Having experienced the effectiveness of Reiki through her own healing it was only natural that Mrs. Takata would want to learn it herself. She studied under Hayashi Sensei for a year before returning home to Hawaii where later, in 1938, she invited Hayashi Sensei and was able to complete all the Reiki levels.

Initially Mrs. Takata did not teach Reiki. She might have taught privately but seems to have concentrated more on healing. It wasn't until 40 years later, in mid 1970s that she began to teach more openly. It must have been really difficult for a Japanese person to introduce something as Japanese as Reiki in Hawaii right after World War II, so it is not surprising that Mrs. Takata waited such a long time.

She taught for only a few years up to her death in 1980, managing to train just twenty-two teachers. The number was not so large but these teachers initiated the spread of Reiki throughout the world and, thanks to them, Reiki is now practiced by millions of people. There are various famous Reiki organizations active today — The 'Reiki Alliance' is led by Mrs. Takata's granddaughter, Ms. Phyllis Furumoto and Dr. Barbara Ray promotes and teaches 'The Radiance Technique®'. These organizations, among others, have been so successful in the promulgation of Reiki that it has now begun to be reintroduced to its homeland, Japan.

REIKI RETURNS TO JAPAN

Reiki has been slowly spreading in Japan once again since 1984 when 'The Radiance Technique®' organization began to hold seminars here. However it wasn't possible to take a teacher's course until 1993 when Mr. Frank Petter, then living in Sapporo, Hokkaido, in the north of Japan started to train Reiki teachers. Since that time a great many people have become teachers and it has gradually become popular here in Japan. We estimate that over 20,000 students have attended these seminars.

Since Reiki started to become re-acknowledged in Japan a number of people have tried to trace its history and thus the existence of the *Usui Reiki Ryoho Gakkai* — the organization founded by Usui Sensei himself — has become known. However this organization is closed to the general public so the original form of Reiki has not been passed down through this source.

As information has been gathered some of the misunderstandings about Usui Sensei and Reiki have gradually been amended. But time passed with core information still missing and Western Reiki teachers concluded that there was no way to learn the original Reiki from the direct lineage of Usui Sensei. Many people were now asking the important question:

'Is it really impossible to learn the original form of Reiki in the way Usui Sensei and Hayashi Sensei taught?'

While Reiki was being reintroduced to Japan, on the other side of the world some others were trying to replicate the original style of Reiki using the book published by *Usui Reiki Ryoho Gakkai, Reiki Ryoho no Shiori.*[3] In spite of their best efforts they could not complete the task effectively as some essential elements were still missing. For example, the symbols and the methods of attunement were not included because these were not handed down via written material.

At this time my mother and I were using Reiki every day completely unaware that it had become so popular or that people were searching for information that we had here.

WHY I STARTED TEACHING JIKIDEN REIKI

Then in 1999 my mother, Chiyoko Yamaguchi, was mentioned in a book written by a well-known Reiki teacher in Japan. This had a profound impact on the Reiki community, much greater than I or my mother could have expected. People were fascinated at the discovery of a woman who had learned directly from Hayashi Sensei and even more amazed by the fact that she had learned it at the age of 17 and had been practicing in her daily life for over 65 years!

Following this publication a great many people started to visit my mother, among them famous Reiki teachers at home and abroad. They encouraged us to start holding seminars replicating those held by Hayashi Sensei in the 1930's.

Initially we rejected the idea. However one day I overheard a colleague from an environmental group talking about Reiki, he claimed that Reiki was 'no big deal' and went on to say that he had taken a one-day seminar but did not feel that he had learned anything useful at all. He relayed the contents of the seminar and I was really amazed to hear that they were so far removed from the great spirit of Reiki. It made me realize that it is important for us to pass on the original teachings of Hayashi Sensei. It was a turning point for me. It was then that my mother and I decided to set up *Jikiden Reiki Kenkyukai* (institute) and start seminars.

I would like to express my gratitude to all the Reiki teachers who gave me encouraging advice motivating me to start doing what I now do.

JIKIDEN REIKI
AND WESTERN REIKI

I am often asked, "What is the difference between *Jikiden* Reiki and Western Reiki?"

Both *Jikiden* and Western Reiki have their roots in Usui Sensei's Reiki. However they are not exactly the same, as Western Reiki has left some elements behind and added various new ideas and practices.

I do not mean that Western Reiki is imperfect or wrong and I understand the reasons why some elements have not survived. It is possible that if the original form had been rigidly adhered to it would have fallen flat in other cultures and only a small number of people may have been blessed with Reiki. It is natural that in different cultures Reiki should spread in different ways for the people with varying cultural backgrounds to accept it. I feel that we shouldn't be focusing on the differences. Instead we need to focus on the universality of Reiki and its incredible healing capabilities.

As I touched on in my preface, I know a Reiki teacher overseas who has been successful helping cancer patients at a hospital. To me, giving one's best effort to help people is the great original spirit of Reiki as passed down by Usui Sensei and Hayashi Sensei. As I see it, the differences in techniques are not as important as attitude, so I believe that it is very important that the original teachings of Hayashi Sensei be passed on, not just in terms of techniques but of the fundamental attitudes and intentions he maintained.

You might have been wondering what 'Jikiden' means. 'Jikiden' is a general term for the Japanese (it is a term often used in traditional Japanese arts) that means 'directly transmitted or passed down from one's teacher' and for us the teacher is

Hayashi Sensei. I named my institute and seminar 'Jikiden Reiki' because I have been trying to replicate as closely as possible the teachings passed down to my mother directly by Hayashi Sensei. I am afraid it is impossible to make it exactly the same as Hayashi Sensei's seminars. However, I have resolved to do my best to complete the mission and I have been reconfirming the content of the seminar not just with my mother but also with my relatives who also often attended Hayashi Sensei's seminars. Moreover, I believe that the most important asset of *Jikiden Reiki* is my mother's 65 years' devotion to Reiki. Cherishing my mother's experience I am determined to further improve myself doing the best job I can as selflessly as possible. I will leave it to your judgment.

Chapter 2:

Reiki and My Family

BIOGRAPHY OF MY MOTHER, CHIYOKO YAMAGUCHI

First of all let me introduce my mother.

Chiyoko Yamaguchi was born in Kyoto on December 18th 1921. Her maiden name was Iwamoto. She was the second daughter in her family and had six siblings.

She lived in Kyoto until the second grade of elementary school when she went to live with her uncle's family in Tezukayama, a suburb of Osaka. This uncle, Mr. Wasaburo Sugano, was the person who brought Reiki into my family. I will elaborate on him later.

She grew up with Mr. Sugano's family because Mr. Sugano did not have any children of his own and Chiyoko's parents had seven. The Suganos had intended to adopt her as their own daughter but this was never realized.

Later, when she was around ten years old, Chiyoko and one of her brothers moved to Ishikawa prefecture, the family's hometown, to live with another family of relatives, the Ushios. After she moved there, she began to hear people around her talking about Reiki all the time. When one of the family members was not well, the others would say that they would give him or her

THE FAMILY TREE OF THE YAMAGUCHIS, THE USHIOS, THE SUGANOS, THE IWAMOTOS

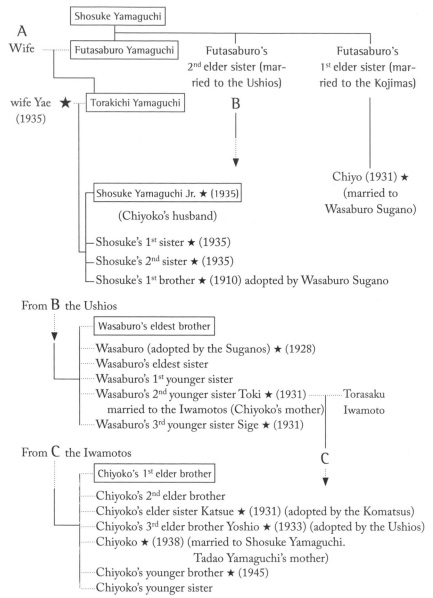

A

Shosuke Yamaguchi

Wife ········ Futasaburo Yamaguchi

Futasaburo's 2nd elder sister (married to the Ushios)

Futasaburo's 1st elder sister (married to the Kojimas)

wife Yae ★ ···· Torakichi Yamaguchi

B

Shosuke Yamaguchi Jr. ★ (1935)
(Chiyoko's husband)

Shosuke's 1st sister ★ (1935)

Shosuke's 2nd sister ★ (1935)

Shosuke's 1st brother ★ (1910) adopted by Wasaburo Sugano

Chiyo (1931) ★
(married to
Wasaburo Sugano)

From **B** the Ushios

Wasaburo's eldest brother

Wasaburo (adopted by the Suganos) ★ (1928)

Wasaburo's eldest sister

Wasaburo's 1st younger sister

Wasaburo's 2nd younger sister Toki ★ (1931) ········ Torasaku
married to the Iwamotos (Chiyoko's mother)   Iwamoto

Wasaburo's 3rd younger sister Sige ★ (1931)

From **C** the Iwamotos   **C**

Chiyoko's 1st elder brother

Chiyoko's 2nd elder brother

Chiyoko's elder sister Katsue ★ (1931) (adopted by the Komatsus)

Chiyoko's 3rd elder brother Yoshio ★ (1933) (adopted by the Ushios)

Chiyoko ★ (1938) (married to Shosuke Yamaguchi.
Tadao Yamaguchi's mother)

Chiyoko's younger brother ★ (1945)

Chiyoko's younger sister

★ Family members who were able to practice Reiki. Year of Reiki initiation in brackets..

Reiki. Reiki was a daily term. Because the Ushios were an affluent family they did not have to work outside to make their living. They always had a lot of servants to work for them at home too. They owned some farmland, which was left in the hands of caretakers, so, instead, they helped other people with Reiki. The Suganos, who in those days were living in Osaka, often stayed with them for a month during summer.

Chiyoko grew up happily in such an affluent family environment. She was lucky that she never had to worry about money in her youth. Even when she got married in 1942 her former foster family, the Suganos, generously helped her prepare for her new life.

FIRST CONTACT WITH REIKI – WASABURO SUGANO

Mr. Wasaburo Sugano, my mother's uncle who treated her like his own daughter, was the key person who brought Reiki into our family. He was a hard working-man from Daishoji, Ishikawa in the North of Japan who moved to Osaka to start his career. He found employment with the paper manufacturer Okura Yoshiten and there he worked his way up to become an executive director of the company. Mr. Sugano's initial interest in Reiki was spurred by the sad deaths of both of his children. His first child died soon after birth and his second at the age of fifteen from tuberculosis (TB), which in those days was considered incurable.

Success, with all the money, power and status that it brings, could not save his children for him. Conventional medicine offered nothing. He was completely helpless. Hearing about *Reiki Ryoho* (treatment) by chance around 1928, his initial interest was prompted by these bitter experiences and it led him to his first Reiki seminar with Chujiro Hayashi Sensei in Sakai, Osaka.

Around this time Hayashi Sensei and his organization, which he called 'Hayashi Reiki Kenkyu-kai', held seminars in Osaka on a monthly basis. Mr. Sugano progressed from the '6th *kyu* (degree)' and then the '5th *kyu*'. He kept on and completed the *Shoden* and *Okuden* levels.[4] 'Kyu' is a set of levels preceding the *Shoden* and *Okuden*. The 'kyu' degrees were given when participants joined a session to experience Reiki. At this stage they were not yet permitted to practice Reiki on others. I hear there were four levels of 'kyu' up to the highest, the 3rd one. After these levels were completed they were allowed to join the main courses—*Shoden* and *Okuden*. I will elaborate upon the differences between the levels in a later chapter.

Mr. Sugano was so impressed with the effectiveness of Reiki that he actively promoted it amongst his extended family and his co-workers in Osaka. Many were invited to Osaka from his hometown Daishoji, Ishikawa to take Reiki seminars. He wanted to give Reiki treatments to his elderly mother in Ishikawa but he was too busy in his business and lived too far away from her so he had his niece, (my mother's elder sister) Katsue, take a seminar in Osaka so she could go and give Reiki to his mother.

Katsue commuted to the seminar from her uncle Sugano's home in an affluent suburb of Osaka for five consecutive days. The lecture lasted only three hours everyday but was followed by a practical treatment session conducted by Hayashi Sensei himself. She fondly remembers that she was able to meet a lot of different people there including some famous *Kabuki* actors. (*Kabuki* is a traditional Japanese theatre and any Japanese person from her generation would have recognized these actors.)

RECOVERING FROM TUBERCULOSIS (TB)

As I mentioned earlier, Mr. Sugano became interested in learning Reiki after the painful experience of losing both of his children to tuberculosis. Later his wife Chiyo also became afflicted with the same illness but fortunately by that time Sugano had already started practicing Reiki. He gave her intensive treatments and she was privileged also to receive treatments from Hayashi Sensei himself. Thanks to this attention she made a complete recovery from TB, which at that time was thought to be incurable.

Naturally through this life-saving experience Mrs. Chiyo Sugano also became enthusiastic about Reiki, even more so than her husband.

This is not the only story of miraculous recovery from TB. Mr. and Mrs. Sugano also helped my mother's elder brother completely recover from tuberculosis. Around that time Japan was in the middle of World War II and her brother was about to be conscripted for military service. He was rejected however because the physical examination revealed that he had TB. He was sent back home to Ishikawa. The Suganos heard about this and invited him to Mr. Sugano's sister's home in Osaka, which was close to their house. They gave him Reiki treatments every day and Hayashi Sensei joined them for some of the treatments. Thanks to their efforts my uncle completely recovered from TB. He regained his health and as a result ended up having to go to war, however he returned home fine and well and lived a healthy life to the age of 67.

In those days TB was considered incurable and it was really hard, not only for the one suffering, but it also weighed on the patient's entire family. If it became known to others in the community, people became afraid of contact with the family. Daughters would be excluded from bridal candidate lists so it was often kept secret. My mother, even as the patient's sister, did not know for a long time that her brother had been infected.

After this Mr. and Mrs. Sugano were completely convinced of the effectiveness of Reiki. From that time on Mrs. Chiyo Sugano taught Reiki to many people in Daishoji, Ishikawa including her

Around 1945 at Hayashi Sensei's memorial service. Chie Hayashi Sensei is the lady in the middle with the glasses, Chiyo Sugano (Chiyoko's aunt) is standing next to her on the right.

relatives. She gave *Reiju* to my father Shosuke Yamaguchi and his mother Yaeko (my grandmother).

After Hayashi Sensei passed away in 1940 Mrs. Sugano helped Mrs. Chie Hayashi, Hayashi Sensei's wife, conduct seminars in Ishikawa. Mrs. Sugano was the main organizer when the memorial service for Hayashi Sensei was held in Daishoji, Ishikawa. I will go into more details of this later.

SETTING UP THE DAISHOJI BRANCH

In Daishoji Ishikawa those who had learned Reiki in Osaka practiced it actively to heal others. Those who were helped became interested in learning it themselves but it was very expensive and very time consuming to go all the way to Osaka to take the course in those days. Mr. Wasaburo Sugano wondered if he could invite Hayashi Sensei to Ishikawa, knowing that he had been traveling around Japan teaching Reiki. He happily accepted the invitation knowing Mr. Sugano had been a trusted and major contributor to the promotion of Reiki. He said he would come if there were more than ten participants.

In 1935 the first seminar was held in Daishoji, Ishikawa. It became a regular event after this and was held twice a year, in spring and autumn. Hayashi Sensei was always welcomed and shown a great deal of hospitality by the locals in Daishoji whenever he visited there. He was always put up in an elegant traditional Japanese health resort near Daishoji. They hired a taxi each day to take him to and from the seminar, which was a rather special way to treat a guest those days. In the first seminar there in 1935 Chiyoko Yamaguchi's elder sister, Katsue, took the *Okuden* level training.

At that time moving up to the next level took more time and effort to practice than it does today. Katsue had previously attended Hayashi Sensei's monthly Reiki seminars held in Osaka

The very first seminar in Ishikawa. In the middle is Hayashi Sensei. The young girl on the left is Chiyoko Sensei's elder sister Katsue.

(the seminars were also held in Tokyo) and progressed step by step from 6th *kyu* to 3rd *kyu* leading to *Shoden*. Students were allowed to participate in the *Okuden* training course only after a lot of practice, which would enable them to feel *Byosen* (problematic areas). (I will elaborate upon this *Byosen* concept in the chapters 3 and 5). However Hayashi Sensei did give an intensive five-day course of both *Shoden* and *Okuden* coupled with longer hours each day when he taught outside Tokyo and Osaka. He did the same in Ishikawa.

Hayashi Sensei traveled all over Japan. As well as in Tokyo and Osaka, he taught Reiki in Aomori, Mie, Wakayama and many other towns. People in those places started to form their own branch organizations. I have established that there were branches in Osaka and Ishikawa at this time and I am certain that there were more in other places but I haven't been able to confirm those yet.

Following *Okuden* the next level was *Shihan-kaku* (or assistant teacher level). At this level practitioners were permitted to teach the *Shoden* course. After *Shihan-kaku* the next level was Shihan (teacher). *Shihans* were instructors who were allowed to teach both the *Shoden* and *Okuden* courses. Mr. Sugano reached *Shihan* around 1933 and in the late 1930s he was permitted by Hayashi Sensei to instruct teachers. My mother Chiyoko learned *Reiju* to become a *Shihan* from Mr. Sugano. She was very young but she had a lot of treatment experience, which qualified her to learn *Reiju*. Later she attended seminars as a *Shihan* and was honored to practice *Reiju* with Hayashi Sensei's wife, Chie Hayashi Sensei.

By the time the first seminar was held in Ishikawa some people had already been granted the *Shihan-kaku* diploma in Osaka. They organized a *Reiju-kai* (attunement session) every month so people were able to receive *Reiju* monthly from those local *Shihan*-kakus even though Hayashi Sensei was not present. By the time Chiyoko Yamaguchi attended her first seminar in 1938 people in Daishoji had already formed their own branch — the Daishoji Branch. She recalls that there were some *Shihans* there.

CHIYOKO YAMAGUCHI'S REIJU EXPERIENCE

As I have mentioned my mother lived with her relatives, the Ushios, from the age of ten. In that family Reiki was practiced daily. Whenever she had some minor ailment like a headache, stomach ache, cold or fever she was given Reiki by her uncle, aunt or her own sister. After the Reiki treatment she always felt better so she hardly ever needed to see a doctor.

Sometimes the neighbors would come to see her sister Katsue for a Reiki treatment. They would always feel better after the treatment and thank Katsue profusely. Chiyoko was continually impressed with Reiki and it was only natural that she would be eager to learn it herself. However her uncle made her wait until she graduated from school. She waited impatiently for that day.

29

The tuition fee for Reiki seminars in those days was 50 yen when the average salaried workers were getting 47 yen a month showing that it was extremely expensive. However Mr. Sugano was convinced that she should take it. He thought it would be most useful for her when she got married and had a family of her own. It would be more worthwhile spending money on the course than spending a fortune on luxurious wedding arrangements[5]. This shows how seriously the family took Reiki.

The great day finally came. On March 13 1938 Chiyoko joined the five-day course of *Shoden* and *Okuden*. Accompanied by her elder sister Katsue she left the house in a brand new *Kimono* (a traditional Japanese garment made of silk) that Mr. Sugano had bought for the occasion. They headed to the house of a member of the Daishoji Branch where the seminar was to be held. The 17-year old girl was very excited but extremely nervous at the same time. From here I would like to use my mother's own words so can you feel the atmosphere.

Chiyoko Yamaguchi at the age of 17

Chiyoko:

"When we got to the house some people were there already. Most of them were much older than I was. Some of the men there were wearing formal attire, which made the atmosphere very serious. My sister Katsue had already been a regular member at the Daishoji Branch so she seemed pretty comfortable but I was totally overwhelmed. I felt a little reassured when I found one of my aunts among the coordinators of the seminar. I remember seeing three rows of six *Zabuton* (a Japanese style cushion for sitting on the floor) and we were each told to sit on one of them in order. I don't really remember the exact number of the participants that day."

She remembered that the coordinators greeted the participants with an explanation of the appropriate manner in which to receive *Reiju* (attunement). Here is how the *Reiju* was done:

Coordinator:
"Firstly the room will be darkened. We ask you to be seated in the *Seiza* posture (formal Japanese sitting style on one's knees) with your eyes closed, sitting up straight and taking care no pressure is put on the lower *Tanden* (a spot three cm lower than the navel).
Please place your hands in *Gassho* (folded hands in prayer style).
Even after your *Reiju* is completed please remain seated quietly until all the participants finish receiving *Reiju*. You are not to leave the seat or to talk."

Chiyoko:
"After the briefing sessions Hayashi Sensei entered the room dressed in *Haori* and *Hakama* (traditional Japanese formal suit type kimono). I had known that Hayashi Sensei was a respected naval officer and I was impressed by his dignified appearance and impressive bearing. A tall man, he appeared to have light shining all around him.
The room was very dark because the shutters were all closed and lights had been turned off.

Chiyoko's first seminar in 1938. The 3rd man in the back row is Hayashi Sensei. Chiyoko Sensei is standing 5th from the right. The 4th girl is her sister Katsue.

With Hayashi Sensei leading, *Go-kai-no-sho* (the five Reiki principles written on the scroll that was hung in the room where the attunements took place) was recited by the participants. The room was so dark that they could not read the words on the scroll. So they followed what Hayashi Sensei read, line by line. They recited the *Gokai* three times.

Occasionally before the *Reiju* he chanted out loud *Gyosei* of the Meiji Emperor (These are traditional Japanese *Waka* poems which, when written by an emperor are specially known as *Gyosei*. For further information about *Gyosei* please refer to Chapter 3). Then the *Reiju* finally began. First we were given *Reiju* by Hayashi Sensei, followed by others who held the *Shihan* (teacher) degree. I remember that there were possibly three *Shihans* but it was so dark that I could not confirm the exact number. Each *Reiju* lasted about five minutes.

After the *Reiju* all the participants came together to form a *Reiki Mawashi* (sitting in a circle, each person laying their hands on the person sitting in front in order to feel the Reiki circulating). Sometimes Hayashi Sensei himself joined the circle and at other times he sat in the center giving instructions to the participants. Hayashi Sensei then went on to explain the theory behind Reiki.

The seminar started at 10 am. In the morning we received one *Reiju*. Then we sat to listen to the lecture given by Hayashi Sensei and we also had a practical training. We gave Reiki to a person lying on the Reiki table, which was made of rattan. For the receiver we used a blanket to cover his or her body and a small cotton towel for the head. The beds were 30 to 40 cm high which helped practitioners sit straight when giving Reiki. We all had a chance to experience being both a giver and a receiver. We had the opportunity to lay hands on different parts of the body of different receivers every day throughout the entire five-day seminar. Sometimes there was an opportunity to give an actual Reiki treatment to someone with an illness who lived close to the venue."

REIKI — A GREAT GIFT FOR A BRIDE TO BRING TO HER NEW FAMILY

Having constantly received Reiki throughout her childhood Chiyoko learned to be a good Reiki practitioner quite quickly. After she took the seminar her foster grandmother at the Ushios told Chiyoko that strong Reiki was radiating from her hands. This remark gave Chiyoko the confidence to treat people in need. She treated a lot of people, especially young children with problems such as burns or bed wetting.

She married in 1942 at the age of 21 and was soon totally convinced of what Mr. Sugano had told her "Reiki would be very helpful and would be a wonderful bridal gift to bring to her husband's family".

Chiyoko:
"After I became pregnant I gave Reiki to my unborn baby. It worked really well and all of my kids were healthy. All four of my children were boys and they often suffered injuries and sometimes got sick. Whenever something happened to them Reiki helped greatly. It was really reassuring for such a young mother in those days. It is like they were brought up with Reiki."

When my mother received *Reiju* for the first time her high school friends ridiculed her. They thought it absurd to spend money on something so intangible and thought it better spent on more substantial things like traveling or kimonos (clothing). Some said they would not buy Reiki at all. They said, "If this kind of hand healing can cure sicknesses why would we need doctors?" The funny thing is that she found the answer to these kinds of remarks through her own experience. She would say, "Indeed we don't need doctors". My mother made every effort to enhance her Reiki energy, to bring it to a level where there was "no need for doctors". In fact I have never seen a doctor since I was a little boy.

Chiyoko:
"Even if you learn such a wonderful healing art, if you don't practice it at all you won't be able to use it when it's needed. It all depends on how seriously you practice what you have learned. My grandmother used to tell me to help others whenever possible. So whenever there was someone who was not well my grandmother would suggest that I give him Reiki and I did so. Thus I have had a lot of surprising experiences with Reiki".

My mother Chiyoko proceeded to the *Shihan* level around 1940. She did this under her uncle, Mr. Wasaburo Sugano's instruction with the permission of Hayashi Sensei. Mr. Sugano by then had

Chiyoko (34 years) with Tadao (3 years)

gained qualification to teach *Reiju* to other people. In those days the *Shihan* degrees were not given in a seminar the way we do today. When a person was ready he or she was able to learn to give *Reiju* privately.

My mother was still very young but she had had a lot of treatment experience and wanted to gain this level because she was leaving for Manchuria with her husband. She thought it would be helpful to know how to give *Reiju* to others. Before she left for Manchuria she met Chie Hayashi Sensei (Hayashi Sensei's wife). Mrs. Hayashi's warm words of encouragement moved her greatly to help people with Reiki in the new place.

LIVING THROUGH THE WAR WITH REIKI

During and after World War II Reiki helped my family through the troubled times. My mother got married in February 1942, a year after Japan became involved in the war. Prior to their marriage my father, Shosuke Yamaguchi, had gone to Harbin in Manchuria to start a business but he came back to Japan temporarily because he fell ill.

After he recovered from the illness they got married and moved to Manchuria, not knowing that they would have to go through a stormy time there because of the war. Without Reiki their life would have been even harder.

In Manchuria my mother gave Reiki treatments to her family and neighbors. They were grateful to her for helping their kids when they had problems like toothache. However it was during their return to Japan that Reiki helped her most.

Chiyoko:
"In those chaotic times normal medical services were not available. One day I happened to get a whitlow. I gave it Reiki constantly and it healed. That greatly renewed my appreciation of Reiki.

Some people who had brought their children from distant places had no choice other than to leave them with Chinese families because either they or the children had fallen ill on the way and they were unable to bring them back home. The local school near my house was packed with Japanese refugees evacuated from far away places.

I saw some children who were starved to the point of madness. They even tried to eat pieces that they pealed off the walls in the school. In the end they died.

There were no doctors or medicine available. As much as possible I tried using Reiki to help people in these situations. I never felt such necessity for Reiki in my life.

Finally I managed to get on board a vessel returning home. I sat in the hold with my two sons for the whole week it took to get back to Japan. There was anarchy on that ship. There were robberies even between Japanese people and the atmosphere was very tense.

People were avoiding one another so it was difficult to practice Reiki there. However I had occasion to use it when kids sitting near me got food poisoning from some old rice, which was the only food available.

I think it was there that I lost all my Reiki documents, including my certificate granted by Hayashi Sensei and the notebooks I had cherished. It was unfortunate but Reiki was alive in my palms and has never been lost. I came back to Japan in good shape thanks to the Reiki in my hands."

SAVING MY FATHER FROM TERMINAL ILLNESS WITH REIKI

In the chaos after the war Chiyoko lost contact with her husband Shosuke Yamaguchi. He was called up for military service in March 1945 and went into battle. Five months later, in August that year, the war ended. However he was interned as a prisoner of war in Siberia for three more years and finally came back to Japan in 1948. Those three years were very hard for my mother because she heard nothing from her husband. She was sure that he was alive however. She believed that, as a Reiki practitioner himself, he would manage to heal himself and help others. Moreover there was one more reason that made her believe that he would be fine. When she sent him distant Reiki she could feel sensations in her palms, which suggested that the receiver was alive. Back then all her family were Reiki practitioners and they also sent Reiki to their husbands, sons and brothers to confirm that they were alive.

After he got back to Japan he went into a military hospital where he had to stay for two years. His doctor told the family that he would not survive long. On the battle field the shock from a blast had caved in a part of the back of his head and cracked his skull. This left him with chronic headaches. We asked one of the best doctors from Kyushu in Southern Japan to help him. The doctor told the family that the operation would cost 30,000 yen, an enormous amount of money back then, and that he could not guarantee that it would help him. Actually the doctor was quite amazed that someone in this condition could still be alive. He also said that my father would not regain full functioning of his brain. He was sorry, but he would not even be able to calculate easy math problems and it would be quite impossible for him to go back to work or deal with difficult tasks. He also mentioned that he would not be surprised if my father's skull broke open like a bowl at any moment. When she heard this news my mother was so shocked that she could not utter a word.

Chiyoko:
"I was totally freaked out. It was as if icy water had been splashed on my back. I did not know how to bring up our

38

young children all by myself. However there were a lot of other people in even worse situations and considering this I pulled myself together and tried to be optimistic. After all, my husband was still responding when I talked to him. If necessary I was willing to be the breadwinner. The most important thing was that my husband was still alive. It encouraged me and with this realization I calmed down."

So everyday my mother gave Reiki to my father's wounded head, as did my father himself. The result was that he became well enough to go back to work even though he still had to use painkillers. He had been a successful businessman in Manchuria and once he regained his health through Reiki he was motivated to be successful again. He took his family to Kyoto where he began again from scratch.

When they came to Kyoto they were penniless. My mother who had been brought up in a wealthy family was miserable at first, but thanks to their business the family managed to make ends meet.

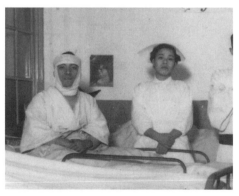

Shosuke Yamaguchi in the Military Hospital
at Yamanaka spa, December 1950

39

A HEALING FAMILY —
THE YAMAGUCHIS

Even before the 20th century and our own Reiki experience there was a healing tradition in my family. Before I go on with my personal Reiki story I will give you a brief idea of my family background.

MY SAMURAI ANCESTORS AND
A JAPANESE TYCOON

One of my ancestors was a feudal lord during the Medieval Period in Japan, and owner of Daishoji castle in the region of Kaga (Ishikawa prefecture today). His name was **Yamaguchi Genbanokami Munenaga.** The family was charged with supervising a large area of land and rendered devoted loyalty to the then ruler of Japan, *Hideyoshi Toyotomi* — a major historical figure who actually brought about the unification of Japan during the warring period in the 16th century. Since Hideyoshi Toyotomi did not leave an adult heir a scramble for power followed his death in 1598. That led to a major battle (*Sekigahara Battle* on October 22nd, 1600). The winner of this battle was Hideyoshi's foremost vassal, *Ieyasu Tokugawa*, who successfully swept away the survivors of the Toyotomis.

Ieyasu Tokugawa started his administration in Edo (now Tokyo) and assumed the old title of *Shogun*[6]. This was the beginning of the long lasting *Tokugawa Shogunate* (also known as the Edo-Period), which marked a big turnaround in the history of Japan. The successful policies of successive Tokugawas enabled them to stay in power for the next 250 years, up until the mid-19th century.

My ancestors' family belonged to the Toyotomi side. Losing a battle fought against *Toshiie Maeda* of the Tokugawa side prior to the Sekigahara Battle, their status then collapsed.

After the defeat some of the family descendents, who had escaped and managed to survive, hid themselves in a small village called Sugao in Daishoji. They were brought up there as the children of the master of that village but they secretly kept the family name. For the next 400 years the family name was passed from generation to generation and it was inherited by my father.

ABOUT THE DRAGONFLIES
ON THE COVER OF THIS BOOK

During the Period of the Warring States in Japan dragonflies were thought to be a lucky sign, which would bring Samurai warriors victory. The ancestors of the Yamaguchis were Samurai and the family back then wore armor emblazoned with images of dragonflies. When my book was published in Japanese someone suggested that we put a picture of dragonflies on the cover to pay respect to the guardian spirit that had protected my ancestors. For the English edition I also asked for them on the cover in the hope that they would help me send this great message to people around the world.

MY FAMILY'S HEALING ROOTS ANCESTORS
BACK IN PREHISTORIC TIMES

Interestingly, it is thought in my family that our ancestors, dating even further back, were a family of *Shinto* priests and healers who used their hands to heal with. It is believed that we originally came from Izumo (which for Japanese is a spiritual region

The tree where the Hakuryujin are believed to reside.
In the left corner is Shosuke Yamaguchi.

and today is known as the Shimane prefecture). I have heard from my relatives that our family name, Yamaguchi, actually comes from the Yamaguchi prefecture next to Shimane where Izumo is located. They were *Shinto* priests in a shrine there for several generations. But when Buddhism emerged the original ancient Japanese *Shinto* was swept away and took refuge deep in the mountains. My ancestors had to abandon it, and this may have been the reason they decided to give up healing to become warriors who would protect people in a different way during the Warring State Period.

From generation to generation my family has believed that the *Hakuryujin* (white dragon gods) have been the family's guardian spirits. The *Hakuryujin*, which consist of a male and a female dragon each holding a golden ball in their mouth, have been protecting my family for more than 2000 years.

In the Yamaguchis' garden in Ishikawa there was a huge tree and *Hakuryujin* were said to live in it. It was said that the *Hakuryujin* showed their appearance only to those who were next in line in the family. My father told me that he saw a white snake in the tree when he was a little boy. Then, after my father passed away, my mother often saw the image of the *Hakuryujin* there.

I believe that the *Hakuryujin* support and have led my mother and me to do what we do today—heal people and teach Reiki.

MY LIFE WITH REIKI

MY CHILDHOOD

I have three elder brothers and all of us were helped by my mother's Reiki whenever we had a problem. One thing I remember vividly is getting my toe caught in the wheel of my father's bike and it almost being torn off. It did not however become serious thanks to my mother giving me a lot of Reiki. Even when I once got a whitlow (a kind of infection on hands or feet caused by germs that get into cuts or hangnails), I did not have to have the nail removed, which was the conventional way to treat such an infection. My mother gave me Reiki. The nurse at the hospital was surprised at how quickly it healed, remarking every time she changed the dressing. It healed within ten days.

In my childhood I picked up many other infections such as tonsillitis, tympanitis (inflammation of the middle ear) and

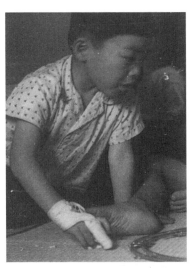

Tadao 6 years old, with the whitlow

they were all cured by Reiki. I was a delicate little boy who got sick quite often, so my mother's Reiki was indispensable to me. I could say that I was brought up on Reiki and thanks to it I did not become a victim of modern medicine. Had my mother not practiced Reiki I might have received excessive medications and ruined my immune system. Because I did not take any medicine my natural healing processes functioned well and in my 20s I grew to be quite healthy.

However in my schooldays life with Reiki was not always easy. As an innocent little boy I was not aware of the social acceptability of Reiki. I talked a lot about it to my teachers and classmates. I remember telling them, "I get my mother to give me Reiki when I have a cold" and, "I will get my mother to give me Reiki because I hurt myself," and so on because it was natural for me to talk like that. But it must have been very strange for those who heard what I had to say. Most of them ridiculed me and I gradually came to understand that I better not talk about Reiki with other people.

REIKI AS MY LIFESAVER

I have had a lot of amazing experiences with Reiki in my life. It has saved me in various situations. I have had four life threatening accidents but each time I miraculously survived by the skin of my teeth. I was not aware of it until recently but I now have no doubt that I have been protected by some invisible being. I believe I owe this blessing to Reiki.

The first accident happened when I was just four years old. I was riding a tricycle on an unpaved street and the front wheel got stuck on something. I was thrown on my face on the gravel path. I vividly remember my vision going white and everything moving into slow motion, and then, silence. I remember seeing the surface of the gravel right in front of me before hitting it.

Strangely I was quite calm. What my mind said was just, "it would be VERY painful to land face first on the ground". Then I literally scraped the ground with my face. Time stood still until my upside down tricycle came into view. Suddenly I was back in reality and I felt pain all over my face.

I cried all the way home. When my mother saw me covered with blood she didn't panic but took me to the bathroom. While I was complaining of great pain my mother gently talked me into letting her help me wash the gravel off my face. She didn't use any disinfectant or medicine but gave me Reiki, covering my face with a cotton towel. A few hours later the pain eased and I fell asleep in the warmth of my mother. This was my very first experience of the impressive efficacy of Reiki treatment. Thanks to my mother's Reiki the painful wounds were healed within a few days and a couple of weeks later there was no trace, no scars.

Tadao 5 years old. Around this time
Chiyoko started giving him Reiju.

The second incident took place during my second year of high school. One day in March I was crossing a street on my bike when a car suddenly exploded from a blind corner and came at me at full speed. I had another experience where everything went into slow motion. I could even clearly see the fear in the driver's eyes. The car hit me and tossed me into the air but my body seemed to have turned somersault and I landed on my feet. Trying to stand up I felt a sharp pain in my right leg. The pain brought me back to my senses and I suddenly found myself surrounded by worried faces and lots of people.

In emergency at the hospital the X-ray showed that I had a bruised calf muscle, which would heal in ten days. It was amazing that I did not have any cracked bones even though my bike was bent V-shape and impossible to repair. During my stay in hospital my mother and the rest of the family came to give me Reiki whenever possible. Thanks to them the swelling reduced and it healed quickly.

The third event happened during the summer holidays when I was 18. I was riding a motorbike along a ridge. Driving a little too fast I spun out and came off. Here again the scenery went blank and into slow motion and I saw my motorbike flying over the top of me in the air. I wound up in the ditch. My torso was stuck between the paddy field and the ridge. After a while I started to feel a piercing pain around the wounds and my whole body began to ache. There was sharp pain all over my body as my friends pulled me out of the ditch. Even though the pain lasted a while it was fortunate that I wasn't badly hurt. Miraculously it was only superficial and I did not need any medical attention. Again, Reiki was there to help me.

The forth accident was the worst and happened when I was thirty-five. One day I got stuck in a big traffic jam on the highway. We were moving so slowly that we were almost at a standstill. Suddenly an eleven-ton truck careened across the centerline and came smashing into my car. At the very moment the truck came

Newspaper article about the traffic accident, October 1987. In the photo you can see my car after the crash.

before my eyes memories of my past flashed in front of me like movie. I thought that this was it. But the thought came to me, "No, I don't want to die yet," and "I can't die yet!" And accompanying these thoughts I saw my wife and kids like a vision on the dashboard.

Next moment I had rolled over onto the passenger seat, arms wrapped around my knees, instinctively knowing that if I had stayed in the driver's seat I would have been crunched up along with my car.

I don't remember the actual moment the truck smashed into my car but the shock was enormous, all the glass from the windshield and other windows shattering into tiny pieces all over me. Momentarily, as before, everything went blank and silent. I wondered if I was already dead. The next moment I was back alive in the terrible scene, people shouting all around me.

The truck had shoved my car into the vehicle behind which then exploded in flames. Realizing that I was still alive I struggled to get out of the car, afraid that it would catch fire from the one behind. The car door was badly crushed and wouldn't open, so I climbed out through the window. Outside the car everyone was panicking. Police cars, fire engines, ambulances and lots of onlookers were gathering in the confusion.

I was taken to hospital by ambulance but luckily I did not have any major injuries and only needed first aid to some minor cuts. Yet my arm was numb from the shock of the crash and my neck ached whenever I moved it. The doctor told me to stay in hospital for a week for observation.

I was even more surprised when I read the newspaper the next day. I had no idea how bad the accident had been until then. It was a thirteen-car pile up. As you can imagine my car was totaled but everyone in my family was happy that I escaped alive from such a major accident. The medical check-up showed no problems so I was able to leave hospital in four days, much earlier than my doctor had expected. I still have no sign of any after effects today.

It is quite miraculous to survive such a major accident. I wonder if Reiki helped me. I strongly believe that Reiki is always there with me. *Reiki Ryoho* (treatment) was passed from the founder, Mikao Usui Sensei down to my mother's uncle, Wasaburo Sugano through Hayashi Sensei. Then with the help of Mr. Sugano it came down to my mother Chiyoko. I grew up with the blessing of Reiki. Now I know why I shouted in my mind at the very moment of the crash — "I can't die yet!" I believe I was given a mission, which is to complete my life's work: handing on *Jikiden Reiki* to coming generations. I have taken this to heart and will strive selflessly to fulfill this mission.

FROM TE-ATE (HEALING WITH HANDS-ON)
TO TE-KAZASHI (HEALING WITHOUT HANDS-ON)

When I was in high school my mother was going through a major turning point in her life. Until then she had been devoted only to Reiki. In those days she was giving Reiki treatment to other people but was too busy to take care of herself and never received Reiki from anyone else. She suffered from neuralgia and one day a neighbor took the opportunity to help her with a certain kind of spiritual *Te-kazashi* (healing without touching) and it was cured. She became curious about what would happen if this spiritual practice was integrated with Reiki energy, so she decided to follow it up. She was also curious about the theoretical aspects of why hands can emit energy to heal people and she thought that she might get to understand it better through the hand healing that this spiritual group promoted.

In the early 20th century there used to be a lot of hand healing arts in Japan, including Reiki. There were quite a few healers within those arts who showed outstanding abilities. Some of them formed spiritual organizations. Originally the ideologies of these movements were often inspiring and eye-opening. I myself was attracted to a movement, which was based on the ministrations of the founder, Mr. Mokichi Okada who was active from 1925 to 1955. I was impressed by his innovative visions for future generations. He was actually one of the first people in the world (the first person in Japan) to advocate organic farming. He also worked on developing methods of hand healing seeking innovative medical procedures. I was in my teens at that time and very impressionable. For me the philosophy of the belief system was really fascinating.

MOKICHI OKADA –
THE FOUNDER OF SPIRITUAL HAND HEALING

For non-Japanese readers I think I should explain a little about this belief system I was once involved in.

As I just mentioned I was interested in a spiritual organization based on the ideas of its founder, Mokichi Okada. In fact there are around thirty organizations officially registered as a religious body with Mr. Okada as founder. If you include the ones which have not registered officially the number would rise to around 100.

I joined three groups among all of these to learn their hand healing methods. Before explaining the spiritual practices I would like to introduce Mr. Okada, the founder. I was greatly inspired by his foresighted theories. He was born in December 1882 in the center of Tokyo. In his youth he ran a variety of businesses and became very prosperous. Despite his success he went through difficult times because he suffered from several diseases. Misfortunes never come singly. Around the same time in 1923 Tokyo was hit by the devastating Great Kanto earthquake and his businesses were seriously damaged. Mr. Okada gave up on his business and was attracted to spiritual life. Later on he devoted himself more and more to these activities. He began a hand healing protocol (it started as a hands-on healing and later it changed to healing without direct touch) and gave treatments, which became quite popular. He opened his hand-healing clinic in Tokyo in 1934. Mr. Okada was very active for many years until he was imprisoned for violation of Medical Law in 1950 having to cease his practice. The law was very strict in those days (and still is today). Unless a person had a medical license he or she was not allowed to even touch another person for 'a treatment'. Hence spiritual healers opted to change their practice to a no touch style of hand healing. They do lay their hands but without directly touching their clients, so it's okay because it is regarded as a religious prayer. This led them to begin placing more emphasis on the spiritual aspects of the belief system rather than practical ones like healing people. Since 1955 when, at the age of 73, Mr. Okada passed away the characteristics of the movement have gradually changed.

MY INVOLVEMENT IN SPIRITUAL ORGANIZATIONS

The first organization my mother and I joined was the one, which was founded by Mr. Okada himself. I was disappointed to discover that, by the time we joined, this organization had already stopped doing the hand healing which Mr. Okada had developed. Yet, there, I was able to learn the fascinating and innovative ideology of Mr. Okada. I was intrigued by what he had predicted about future. He forecast, saying "the time will certainly come when there is tons of food in front of us but we won't be able to eat it", and this is already happening today — he was forecasting the problems created today by agrichemicals, food additives, bird-flu (which is now very serious especially in Asian countries), BSE, carp herpes etc all of which generate inedible food. He was one of the first people to strongly advocate organic farming, a very advanced idea those days.

Even though I could not learn their hand healing method I was very happy to study a variety of material and books still in their library on practical aspects of life written by Mr. Okada. However I was no longer interested in the activities of the organization itself so I left after a few years.

The second one I joined was a group that still practices the Okada style of hand healing. They had developed it in their own way and they rarely spent any time on actual treatments. Even when they did, only a few minutes were spent on a treatment to the receiver's head while the other parts of the body were skipped completely. They placed no great emphasis on the healing of diseases. Their main concern was to acquire as many followers as possible so that the organization would prosper.

I felt sorry for people who joined this organization seeking to cure their diseases, for their needs were not fulfilled. My mother felt the same way and she gave them Reiki whenever possible and it worked well. She didn't tell them that she was using Reiki instead of the spiritual hand healing but her treatments worked wonderfully. Her superiors made her a teacher to take advantage of her healing ability in advertising the organization. However later on they discovered that she had been using Reiki and they banned her from using it on members. We started to lose interest in working there, as the ideas and the ideology of the group were not compatible with our understandings so we gradually stopped participating. A few years later I had the opportunity of contacting people from another branch of the same group. The original reason I was attracted to this sect was still in place and they still cherish and teach the original ideas of Mr. Okada and his style of hand healing. First I got all the publications I could from them and read them thoroughly. I was very excited reading for the first time inspiring articles written by Mr. Okada himself. I also found information I had been looking for so desperately — about his highly effective hand healing method. This motivated me to study with the group.

My mother and I participated in some of their activities and I managed to acquire a lot of valuable knowledge, particularly regarding promoting environmental awareness. One project I joined involved making slides based on the well-known book 'Silent Spring' by Rachel Carson. Another was to help farmers in the Gifu prefecture grow vegetables organically and I took part in selling their vegetables. I followed these activities because they were given as assignments by the spiritual group, but what I learned there affected me profoundly. Concepts took deep root in me and my involvement in environmental activities today is surely based on what I learned there.

It was quite rare back then for a youngster to be involved in such projects so I was given a lot of encouragement. I was fortunate to become friends with people with similar motivations — helping people. It was a precious and wonderful period of my youth.

However Mr. Okada's ideas were well ahead of the times and it was still difficult to get ordinary people to accept them, so the group's activities were quite limited. I have had the same experience with Reiki. It has taken a lot of patience trying to get the society to accept the wonderful legacy of these past teachers. In this group I found it difficult to simultaneously practice Reiki and devote myself to the spiritual activities, their rules were so strict. So I decided to leave them even though I was grateful for being allowed to acquire such valuable information.

I am still inspired by Mr. Okada's work. There are many similarities between his hand healing and Reiki since both are energy healings using the hands.

They do sound very similar but I would like you to understand that Reiki is not a spiritual sect. Usui Sensei did not start it as a religion and Hayashi Sensei did not develop it into a spiritual body either. They passed it down purely as one of the folk medicines. Some people have asked me if I ever mix up Reiki and spiritual hand healing since I used to practice it. I have never mixed them up. My main root is Reiki, so even when I was actively involved in the groups I never stopped practicing it. They might look somehow similar but their fundamental ideas are completely different. It is impossible for these two healing arts to be confused because the way in which we connect to the energy source is completely different in each of them. I respect each of them individually and I have never been tempted to meld them together in anyway.

TACKLING ENVIRONMENTAL ISSUES AND IMPROVING ALTERNATIVE MEDICINE

After finishing with these spiritual organizations I joined Japan's biggest NGO, 'Network Chikyu-mura' (Earth Village, contact: http://www.earthvillage.jp) lead by Mr. Yoshiyuki Takagi. I became secretary general of its Kyoto office and worked there on global environmental issues. It evolved into a branch organization called 'Network Mirai GO' (Network for the Future) dedicated to educating the public. It is now temporarily adjourned but for a time it was very active. We invited environmental specialists to teach and held workshops on such topics as global issues, applying useful microorganisms, organic agriculture and the importance of a healthy diet. During those four years we featured more than 100 lecturers. Once in a while there was a major event with between 300 and 500 people attending.

Recently we invited a very popular singer, the tenor Tsutomu Arakawa, who has been blind since he was a baby but has had an amazing life, which inspired us so greatly. His singing has touched people's hearts. We were lucky to have him with us. This 'talking concert' was co-organized by the NGO 'Network Mirai GO' and 'Jikiden Reiki Kenkyukai (institute)'. It was a great success with more than 600 people attending. I hope to further work on environmental issues within the network at the same time as working constructively to popularize Reiki.

REALIZATION OF HOW WONDERFUL REIKI REALLY IS

In the late 90's I became curious about other systems of alternative medicine and took some short introductory courses in chiropractics and reflexology. I also got an instructor's license for I.H.M.Inc (International Hado Membership contact: http://

55

www.hado.net/) lead by Masaru Emoto who is quite well known in the West today for his photographs of Water Crystals. (More on Mr. Emoto in Chapter 4) I have sought to deepen my knowledge by taking courses whenever and wherever possible. It might sound as if there is no consistency in my progress but it makes complete sense to me. Certainly I have been involved in many things starting with Reiki, moving on to spiritual groups, followed by local environmental issues, global environmental issues and alternative medicine. But from these wanderings I have returned once again, refreshed, to Reiki. The experience has only served to make me even more appreciative of Reiki. I came to understand how simple yet powerful Reiki really is.

It is a very effective alternative medicine. It treats physical illnesses. Reiki is also very effective in treating psychological problems even though many people think this is something only religion should deal with.

It has such a lot of possibilities. I strongly believe that Reiki can also be effective even in dealing with environmental issues because it can lead us to live a more natural life. I am pleased to note that more and more people are tending this way recently and with the opportunity to discuss these environmental issues at conventions I have had a chance to talk to visionary medical doctors about holistic medicine.

Reiki, which is very simple and effective, needs no tools. It is not an outdated thing from the past but a necessary and wonderful method of treatment in this new millennium. Of that I have no doubt.

CHIYOKO YAMAGUCHI'S PEACEFUL DEPARTURE IN 2003

My mother Chiyoko had lived with Reiki since she was very young and when we started teaching in Kyoto in 1999 she was always there in the seminar. It must have been really hard for her in her old age but she always joined in, giving *Reiju* to the participants up until June 2003, two months before she passed away.

She even traveled to Tokyo with me every month for seminars, hard for an 80-year old lady. It's a long train ride from Kyoto to Tokyo but the seminar participants were always so happy to receive *Reiju* from her that she never wanted to disappoint them. It worried me to see her so exhausted at the end of each session and I suggested that I should go to Tokyo alone. At first she agreed but immediately retracted, saying "I am going to Tokyo as long as my body functions!" I told her that she needn't go because anyone who desperately wanted her *Reiju* could come to Kyoto, but she became really stubborn and insisted on going.

Chiyoko decided then to take better care of her health while she was away from home. Beginning with the next trip to Tokyo she took a small rice cooker along to cook her rice porridge. This would be better for her digestion because she found the food and the water in Tokyo very different and never got used to it. After the seminar she would go back to the hotel and cook her simple healthy meal. Later I discovered that her stomach had not been functioning well at that time. I regret that I did not notice her problem but she never told me about it, which is so typical of her. She never wanted others to worry about her.

She continued to make the trip to Tokyo each month up until May 2003. I respect enormously that she never complained about those trips even though they must have exhausted her. She would simply say that she didn't want to disappoint the participants. While this was her main reason I do suspect that she might not have completely trusted her son (me!) as a teacher and had not yet wanted to leave the seminar entirely in my hands.

Her final seminar was the one held in Kyoto in June 2003. She was fine until then and was already planning the Tokyo trip the following month. However when we were packing for Tokyo she experienced unbearable pain in her gallbladder, which was actually an old problem that had first affected her in her early 60s. She had almost forgotten about it. At the time, thanks to Reiki, she had managed to avoid an operation. (My mother really did not want to lose her gallbladder because she had heard that if she did she would have to give up oily food. She simply loved her deep fried *Tempura!*) This time again she gave herself Reiki and the pain eased considerably. She had no intention of canceling the trip to Tokyo so I had to talk her into staying home. Her pain must have been pretty bad because at the last minute she finally gave in.

When I got back from Tokyo I found my mother in hospital. She had wanted me to focus on the seminar and had told my family not to let me know until I returned. She thought she would be out of hospital quickly and told me not to tell anybody because it would make people unnecessarily worry about her. Yet the pain got worse and the doctor wanted to operate. I was not sure what to do. Mother had often said that she would never have any operations and would prefer to die naturally. Some of our family thought we should consider giving modern medical technology a chance, but before we came to a decision the doctor found that her liver and heart were not strong enough to undergo a major operation. I was really surprised at how serious her condition was considering how active she had been right up until the time she was hospitalized. From then on she became progressively weaker. I did not spread the word but some folk found out that she was ill and came to the hospital to give her Reiki. She began to realize how blessed she was and she was very grateful that people were willing to help her. Many of her students sent her distant Reiki at 10 o'clock each morning, which she looked forward to receiving.

The doctor said that she could not last long. My mother was aware of this also, especially when her relatives and grandchildren were coming from far away to gather in her hospital room. Yet she seemed more anxious about the Reiki seminars than her own condition. She kept telling me what to do whenever I visited her, "You don't have to be here to look after me. Go back home to prepare for the seminars!" and "Don't cancel any seminars because of me!" She also told me to make her funeral private and not to bother any of the Reiki students by letting them know about the ceremony. Even when she was in such a critical condition she cared more about other people than about herself.

Her last moments were very peaceful and without the scars of surgery. She passed away as she fell asleep with her loved ones around her. I held out her hand to all her grandchildren and had her give them the last *Reiju*. I am certain that it was the best way for her to end her long life, as a Reiki practitioner. I wished she could have lived longer but I was also moved by her beautiful and peaceful departure.

She had told me to make her funeral private but I decided to make it public. One of the attendants at the funeral had a vision of my mother standing there next to me bowing to greet everyone, asking each person to support me and *Jikiden Reiki*. This delighted me and made me smile because it was so typical of her.

She passed away early in the morning of 19th August 2003. On that day I had planned to give a seminar in Kyoto so, as she had instructed me, I did not cancel even though I almost burst into tears each time I mentioned her name. During that seminar some of the participants told me that they could feel my mother's

Reiju. Hearing the news my good friend Frank Arjava Petter called me from Germany that day and also told me he had felt her in the seminar he was conducting there.

I am sure she is always watching over me. She will show up in my dreams to have a word with me if I do something wrong.

Thank you, mother!

Chiyoko Yamaguchi in spring 2003

Chapter 3:

Basic Reiki Knowledge

AWAKENING TO REIKI – THE ENLIGHTENMENT OF USUI SENSEI

The previous chapter focused on the experiences of my mother and her family, now in this chapter I would like to review the history of Reiki from a broader perspective, based on material in the keeping of my mother's family.

Mikao Usui Sensei the originator of *Reiki Ryoho* (treatment) was born in Taniai Mura (now Miyamacho), Yamagata-gun, Gifu on August 15 1865. He traced his descent from the family of *Chiba Tsunetane*[7]. In his youth Usui Sensei traveled overseas to broaden his experience and expand his knowledge. He was not a rich man, struggling to make a living, often changing jobs and working in various fields as a civil servant, company employee, journalist, political secretary and even a religious missionary and a counselor working to rehabilitate prisoners.

Broad experience enabled him to view the world from a variety of perspectives and he came to ask himself the ultimate question, "What is the true purpose of life?"

After a great deal of profound thought and reflection and having studied history, medicine, Buddhism, Christianity, psychology, asceticism, prophesy and physiognomy to name but a few, Usui Sensei reached the conclusion: "The ultimate purpose of life is to attain **'An-Jin Ryu-Mei'**[8] that is to say, the "state of complete peace of mind or complete stillness".

It led him to study *Zen* Buddhism in an attempt to attain this state. However despite practicing asceticism for three years he could not achieve enlightenment. He became desperate and asked his *Zen* master, whom he greatly respected, for advice on how to train himself to attain what he so greatly desired. His master replied immediately saying, "Well, maybe you should experience death."

This was a great surprise to Usui Sensei and caused him to wonder if that was it—maybe his life was over. So in March 1922 he gave up on life, hid himself in a retreat on Mt Kurama, a mountain just outside Kyoto and started fasting. This fast was not a training as has often been indicated in Reiki books published in the West. It was simply done as a preparation for death. It was in March 1922 that he began it.

Mount Kurama

At midnight during his third week of fasting Usui Sensei suddenly felt a powerful shock in the center of his brain, as if he had been struck by lightning. He lost consciousness. After several hours he came to and woke to find dawn breaking. To his surprise he was feeling refreshed in a way he had never felt before. During this incident divine Reiki energy penetrated his body and soul. As the cosmic energy and his own energy resonated together he came to realize, "The Universe is me — I am the Universe." He had finally achieved the enlightenment he had so long pursued.

FOUNDING AND EXPANDING USUI REIKI RYOHO

Having attained enlightenment Usui Sensei ran joyously down the mountain. On the way he tripped over a rock and ripped off his toenail. He laid his hand on the toe and to his surprise the pain disappeared, the bleeding stopped and the toe was healed. This so amazed him that he rushed back to the *Zen* temple to bring the news to his master who had once told him to experience death. The *Zen* master confirmed that what Usui Sensei had achieved on the mountain was enlightenment. The master also guided him to use the healing ability he discovered on the mountain to heal people and to lead them to enlightenment though the healing.

Usui Sensei was utterly convinced. On his return home he tried it with his family and finding that it produced great results decided to share this blessing with others. After experimenting he developed a method that would enable him to pass on this wonderful ability to other people. This method is now known as 'Shin-Shin Kai-Zen Usui Reiki Ryo-Ho' or 'The Usui Reiki Treatment Method for Improvement of Body and Mind.'

A month after his enlightenment on Mt Kurama Usui Sensei moved to Aoyama-Harajuku in central Tokyo and set up 'Usui

Reiki Ryoho Gakkai' (a study institute). He began teaching openly, conducting seminars which became extremely popular.

I would like to introduce a part of "Reiki Ryoho no Shiori" published by *Usui Reiki Ryoho Gakkai* so that you can get a feeling for the atmosphere back then.

This is a part of the question and answer section. The questions are answered by Usui Sensei.

Q: What is *Reiki Ryoho?*
A: I believe the purpose of Usui *Reiki Ryoho* is to help people fulfill their lives in peace and happiness. To give them great physical and psychological health and to enhance the happiness of those around them by healing them when they are in poor health.

Q: What is Usui *Reiki Ryoho* effective for?
A: It is successful in treating all kinds of illnesses, both physical and psychological.

Q: Does Usui *Reiki Rhoho* only heal sicknesses?
A: No, as well as being very effective in treating physical illness it is useful for physical weakness and for psychological problems including trauma. It is also effective for less severe problems such as timidity, indecisiveness, nervousness etc. Once these problems are resolved you will find yourself in the divine state of mind of Buddha. You will be able to free yourself to heal others and this will bring happiness to you and those you treat.

Q: Shouldn't such healing power belong only to a select few and not be something acquirable through training?
A: All living things possess this incredible ability — plants, trees, insects, animals and humans. Human beings are spiritually the highest in all creation and have the most remarkable

power. Usui Reiki Rhoyo simply embodies this power and makes it available to everyone.

Q: Then you seem to be suggesting here that anyone can be initiated to Usui *Reiki Ryoho*, aren't you?
A: Yes. Anyone with common sense can acquire this spiritual ability to heal diseases, either their own or other's, without fail after a few days of initiation. It doesn't matter whether you are a man, a woman, a great scholar or even illiterate. I have initiated more than a thousand people up to now and no one has failed to acquire it after they have completed *Shoden*. It is quite natural for you to have these doubts about how it might be possible to acquire such ability. It is generally thought to be very difficult for ordinary human beings to heal diseases. However the beauty of the spiritual healing method that I have created is that it makes this possible.

I hope this helps you understand Usui Sensei's view on Reiki.

In those days at *Usui Reiki Ryoho Gakkai* Reiki initiation was given at a *Syuyo-kai* or what we call today a 'seminar' where they would receive *Reiju,* or an attunement. There, students were trained to pursue their spiritual development through healing themselves and others. *Reiki Ryoho* was taught in three levels — *Shoden, Okuden* and *Shinpiden*.

In September 1923 the Great Kanto Earthquake demolished Tokyo injuring a large number of people. Usui Sensei rushed to give Reiki treatments to people in the devastated area. To give treatments to many people at the same time he used his eyes and feet in addition to his hands.

The *Usui Reiki Ryoho Gakkai* grew rapidly as an organization and their center quickly became too small. A new center was built in Nakano, Tokyo, and opened in February 1925. As their fame spread all over the country, in a lot of areas new branch centers were established. On request Usui Sensei visited many places in Japan in order to popularize Reiki. However on March 9 1926 in Hiroshima during one of his Reiki trips Usui Sensei collapsed and died quite suddenly.

USUI REIKI RYOHO GAKKAI TODAY

Usui Sensei is said to have had approximately 2,000 students between 1922 and 1926. After he passed away his most prominent students succeeded him to run the organization named *Usui Reiki Ryoho Gakkai* or 'the Gakkai'.

Among these prominent students there were several people from the Japanese Navy. The second president, Mr. Juzaburo Ushida, and the third, Mr. Kanichi Taketomi were both Rear Admirals in the Navy. The fifth president Mr. Hoichi Wanami was a Vice Admiral. Mr. Chujiro Hayashi who taught Reiki to my mother was himself a Captain. The Navy adopted Reiki because it was useful on long voyages. On warships space was very limited so they used Reiki instead of other more cumbersome medical equipment.

However after Japan lost the war this relationship between Reiki and the Navy backfired. It resulted in restrictions for the activities of the *Gakkai*. The General Headquarters (GHQ) of the US decided to ban all Eastern medicine and force the Japanese to use modern Western medicine only. The Acupuncturist Society lobbied against the GHQ and some folk medicine groups won lawsuits and were able to regain their right to practice. Reiki on the other hand had to halt all official activities because of its connection to the Navy. Practically this closed the door to the public.

The *Gakkai* still exists and it is said to have 300 to 400 members now. It is however quite difficult to obtain membership without an existing member's introduction and unanimous approval of the members. I have also heard said that they aren't even allowed to give Reiki treatments to non-members. The characteristics of the *Gakkai* today seem very different from those in Usui Sensei's day. It is not very active now but when you consider history this change was inevitable.

CHUJIRO HAYASHI SENSEI AND HAYASHI REIKI KENKYUKAI (INSTITUTE)

Usui Sensei trained 20 *Shihans*[9] to replace him suggesting he had known he would not live long. 19 *Shihans* out of 20 gathered on January 16th 1926 to have a *Reiju kai* (attunement session), which was to be the last gathering with Usui Sensei in attendance. Usui Sensei passed away soon after this event.

One of the people attending this gathering was Chujiro Hayashi Sensei, respected teacher of my family. I am publishing for the first time this very precious photo taken at the event. It shows that there were 20 *Shihans*. Hayashi Sensei is the younger looking man on the left hand end of the first row. (Actually he was the youngest of them all. He was 47).

Hayashi Sensei was born in Tokyo on September 15th 1879. He fought in the Russo-Japanese War in 1904 and was appointed Director of Ominato Port Defence Station in 1918. He was a naval doctor and his final status was Captain in the Japanese Navy.

Hayashi Sensei was initiated to *Shihan* and certified by Usui Sensei in 1925 and was qualified to teach the whole course of Reiki. Usui Sensei encouraged Hayashi Sensei to study further using his medical knowledge. He founded his own institute, which he called *The Hayashi Reiki Kenkyukai* (institute), independent from the *Usui Reiki Ryoho Gakkai,* in order to promote Reiki to a wider population. Before war broke out Hayashi Sensei practiced Reiki in his own clinic in Shinano-machi in Tokyo. His clinic was quite large and he was very active. It had 8 Reiki tables and 16 practitioners. As I mentioned in Chapter 2, Hayashi Sensei held *Reiju-kai* (attunement sessions) in Osaka and Tokyo on a monthly basis and he visited other places upon invitation.

Here I would like to introduce some precious material from that time. This is a newspaper clipping of an interview with Mr. Shouou Matsui (1870-1933), a well-known playwright in the early 20th century.

Usui Sensei and 20 Shihans, January 16th, 1926. Transcription of the Japanese writing, top line: Shin Shin Kai Zen Usui Reiki Ryoho Reiju-sha Ichido (Reiju-sha Ichido: Full members of attuners). Bottom line: Taisho 15 nen 1 gatsu 16 nichi, January 16, 1926 (Taisho is the era after Meiji).

In the interview, entitled 'A treatment method to cure all diseases', Mr. Matsui talks about Reiki and mentions Hayashi Sensei by name.

"I was initiated into Reiki by Mr. Chujiro Hayashi who is a Captain in the Navy. Mr. Hayashi was a caring man and very down to earth. I could call him a born healer. He gives treatments to people each morning and gives a Reiki seminar five days every month." (from the "Sunday Mainichi" March 4th 1928 issue)[10]

This is a short note about Hayashi Sensei but it endorses the activities of *Hayashi Reiki Kenkyukai*. There is a lot of controversy about how Hayashi Sensei died. Many people wonder if he really committed *hara kiri* as reported in some books. Actually, it is true that he killed himself but it was an honorable death. He had gone to Hawaii in the critical period just before war broke out. For a high ranking ex-navy officer it was a very risky thing to do. He must have been aware of the risk but he was so determined that he went ahead. When the Japanese navy authority called on him to give information about Hawaii before Japan attacked Pearl Harbor he did not cooperate. Knowing that he would not escape without severe punishment, which would have had a major effect on his family, he chose an honorable death.

After his death on May 11, 1940 his wife, Mrs. Chie Hayashi, took over the *Hayashi Reiki Kenkyukai*. She continued traveling all over Japan in her husband's place. She came to the Daishoji Branch in Ishikawa, my family's hometown, a couple of times each year. In 1941 a memorial service for Hayashi Sensei was held there and it became an annual event in the following years. After World War II Chie Hayashi Sensei temporarily stopped visiting Daishoji but resumed the visits in 1950. Even during her absence the local *Shihans* continued *Reiju-kai* (attunement sessions). Most of the participants in those sessions have now passed away.

Hayashi Sensei had two children but they did not continue in his organization. During their childhood they must have felt lonely, for Hayashi Sensei was away from home almost all of the time traveling to promote Reiki. This may be one of the reasons why they were not willing to carry on their father's institute. The *Hayashi Reiki Kenkyukai* died after Chie Hayashis Sensei's stopping her teaching activities.

At Hayashi Sensei's memorial service, around 1942. In the middle is Chie Hayashi Sensei, Chiyoko Sensei stands in the first row at the left. At this time she had already been given permission to give Reiju by Hayashi Sensei.

HAYASHI SENSEI'S LECTURES IN THE REIKI SEMINARS

My mother recalls Hayashi Sensei's lectures very well. She has vivid recollections of Hayashi Sensei working hard to make his lectures easy to understand and it certainly worked for her. He did not spend too long on lecturing but spent more time on practical training for Reiki treatments. He encouraged the participants to develop sensitivity in their hands, giving suggestions on how to do it. He placed more importance on practice than on theory, as did Usui Sensei.

My mother took notes on Hayashi Sensei's teachings and read them over and over while she practiced Reiki on her family. Understanding the lectures was not so hard for her because she already had a good understanding from her uncle and aunt.

Unfortunately those notes were lost on the way back from Manchuria. She does however remember the gist of the seminars quite clearly. Let me introduce what Hayashi Sensei used to teach in the seminars:

- *Diseases today – more complicated symptoms:*

  Kami (divine being) or universal intention created a 'perfect' world for the human being, which is the crown of all existences. With the development of civilization we are living more and more comfortably and conveniently, and many of us no longer have to worry about food, clothing or shelter. However it is clear that we now have more unsolvable problems than ever before. Psychological problems have become more serious and diseases have become more complicated. There are many terminal illnesses that conventional medicine cannot treat despite developments in medical science.

- *What is a 'Natural healing process'?*

  Human beings possess their own natural cleansing process or healing power. This enables them to cure themselves of their illnesses. Actually these illnesses in themselves are not harmful. For example when we have a cold we develop a fever. The heat from the fever kills the germs, which will be removed with the toxins from our bodies via natural waste systems, hence it is considered a 'natural cleansing process'. Today we even mistakenly believe that we have completely recovered from an illness when in fact the pain only has been eased by some palliative.

- *Activating your own natural healing process by Reiki:*

  It is more important for us to use our own natural healing process to be rid of the underlying problems than to rely on medicine. However in this modern world most people's natural healing powers are unable to function effectively. Reiki practitioners receive energy from the universe and this energy is amplified and passed to patients via the laying on of hands.

  Put simply, Reiki awakens the natural healing powers we all possess but which lie dormant, untapped.

- *Metaphors Hayashi Sensei used in his lectures*

  1. The Muddy Stream...
  Hayashi Sensei often used the image of a 'muddy stream' when explaining the natural cleansing process.
  When you look at the surface of the water it looks clean and clear. However when you stir it the mud from the bottom is brought to the surface making the water cloudy and muddy. If you remove the mud floating on the surface the stream will appear to be clear although some mud will have sunk back down to the bottom. Repeat this process enough times and the muddy stream will eventually be reborn as a clear one.
  By the same process Reiki stirs and removes toxins from our system. After receiving a Reiki treatment, initially a person's condition may appear to become worse because the toxins have come to the surface but this should not be seen as a problem. It is merely a part of the natural cleansing process.

  2. The Finest Paper...
  Hayashi Sensei also used another metaphor. The effects of Reiki are like slowly peeling off sheets of the finest paper, so it is important to continue until recovery is complete. For acute problems the immediate effects of Reiki are easy to see. However chronic illness, although it takes more time, can be

cured too. Once you are able to feel *Byosen* (problematic areas) you will agree that the effects of Reiki are like slowly and gently peeling off sheets of the finest paper until the healthy being is revealed.

病腺
THE LECTURES ON BYOSEN —
FEELING THE ACCUMULATION OF TOXINS

Hayashi Sensei also gave lectures about 'Byosen', which is a very important element in the practice of Reiki. Here I would like to explain it.

The word *Byosen* consists of two characters 病 *Byo* and 腺 *Sen*. *Byo* means ill or toxic. *Sen* means a 'lump', which disturbs the flow of body and the flow of energy. So the word *Byosen* means a lump of toxins, which creates a blockage causing all the flows to stagnate, leading to a poor internal environment from which we are prone to develop an illness.

In most cases *Byosen* starts around the kidneys and spreads to the area between the shoulder blades, the shoulders, armpits, neck and to all the joints of the body. Many of us have stiff shoulders but we don't take these problems very seriously. We tend to think symptoms like stiff shoulders are minor and take no precautions at all. Actually they are early signs of illness that our body is sending us.

More specifically *Byosen* describes the areas that accumulate toxins (usually lactic acid or nitric acid). It usually accumulates where we use our body a lot daily such as joints, neck, shoulders, and internal organs. The toxins work like glue sticking together adjoining muscles and organs and causing their functions to deteriorate. The breakdown of accumulated toxins needs energy and our hands have the ability to sense the area of the blockage.

After receiving *Reiju* (attunement) you will be able to feel unique sensations in your hands when you lay them on the part of the body, your own or someone else's that has *Byosen*. The sensations will gradually change through the effect of Reiki. The stiffness of the body will disappear accordingly. Let me touch on the levels of the sensations.

LEVELS OF BYOSEN

Byosen has its peaks and troughs and is divided into five levels. When you lay your hands on *Byosen* you will feel…

1. *On-Netsu* (Warmth)
When your hands are placed on a stiff part of a receiver's body you will sense warmth (1st level), which is slightly higher than the usual body temperature.

2. *Atsui-On-Netsu* (Intense Heat)
It will be followed by more intense heat (2nd level).

3. *Piri-Piri Kan* (Tingling Sensation)
If the stiffness in the body is even more serious your hands will have a tingling sensation in the palms or fingertips. Some people describe this as "numbness" and others as "electric vibration."

4. *Hibiki* (Throbbing Sensation)
Hibiki is a pulse-like sensation in your hands, which indicates that you can actually feel the Reiki stimulating blood vessels, causing them to expand and contract. At this time the blood circulation is activated and the blood begins to flow more smoothly.

5. *Itami* (Pain)
Itami means a pain, which tells you that the receiver's *Byosen*, is quite serious. If the problem is more serious, your hands

will feel more painful. Pain can move from your palm to the back of your hand, to your wrist and gradually to around the elbow area. Sometimes it stops there and at other times it may move up to your shoulder. After the pain eases, the tingling sensation you felt also simultaneously decreases. When they experience this pain some people become worried about being affected by negative energy from the receiver, but this is not possible so do not worry unnecessarily. Taking your hands off the receiver can easily relieve the pain although occasionally it still continues for a while.

The *Byosen* sensation becomes increasingly strong until it peaks out and slowly becomes weaker. During one treatment of 60-80 minutes it will peak two or three times. It is as if you are repeatedly climbing a mountain. It becomes less each time. The receiver should start to feel better at this point.

To feel the changes clearly it might take some experience but it doesn't take too long if you practice Reiki daily. Some people will first sense *Byosen* immediately after the first *Reiju* (especially those who have done some meditation, breathing discipline, yoga or Qigong exercises) and others take more time. However, in *Jikiden Reiki* seminars most participants get some sensations, even slight, by the end of the three-day course. Hayashi Sensei encouraged everybody to practice in order to make his or her hands more and more sensitive to *Byosen*.

He emphasized the concept of *Byosen* throughout the seminars. While Hayashi Sensei's seminar was focused more on practical training than on theoretical lectures his lectures were however also very important. He would show an anatomical chart to give an understanding of the functions of each organ and the application of Reiki depending on the person's symptoms. Today in *Jikiden Reiki* seminars I tell the participants what my mother learned from Hayashi Sensei. I also spend time explaining how sickness begins and heals, using under-

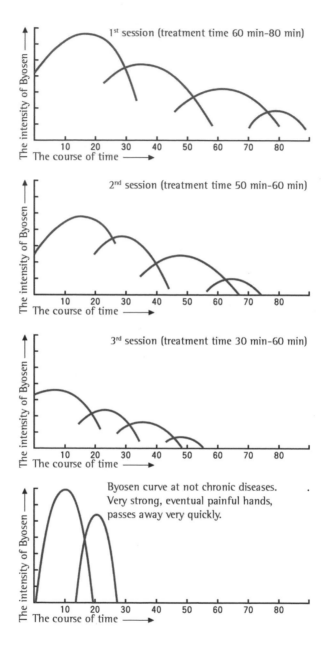

How the feeling of Byosen changes (during three different sessions)
While practicing you will be able to better evaluate the stages.

standings I gathered from my mother and my own past studies. I emphasize how well our body is structured and that we have a natural cleansing ability. I would like to introduce some of the concepts relating to this.

SHIZEN JOKA RYOKU – THE NATURAL CLEANSING ABILITY OF OUR BODY

Our body has the ability to eliminate toxins naturally. When a lot of toxin accumulates the body starts to experience minor reactions and minor symptoms appear. So a minor sickness such as a cold should not be taken as a bad thing. A cold will help the process of elimination of toxins. However in Japan we often say, "A cold is the cause of all serious illnesses," and we tend to think it is better to kill the symptoms by taking medicine in the early stages. By taking such medicines we unwittingly arrest the natural cleansing process. Taking medicine doesn't actually cure the cold but rather it pushes the problem deeper. Rather it would be better to have our immune system activated. So actually it is important to see a minor sickness as a natural way of cleansing the system.

There are two stages in the body's natural cleansing process:

1. In the first stage the system collects toxins from around the body as it prepares to eliminate and deposits them in certain places where there may be a problem (because they are weaker) or where the parts of the body move often (the shoulders for example). When you lay hands on these areas of accumulated toxins your hands will feel *Byosen* sensations. This is regarded as the very first sign of cleansing. It is very effective to give Reiki to these areas at this stage, for this will boost the natural cleansing process.

77

2. The second stage indicates that the body has a lot of toxins to eliminate which have been deposited in one of these areas (as in stage 1) and is preparing to release them from the system. If the body is functioning well the person will get a cold, fever, sickness, rash or diarrhea as an immune response. These ailments allow the body to excrete toxins and return to health. This is the second sign of cleansing taking place. However if chemicals (medicines) are introduced the process is disturbed and this often results in unnatural pain and other negative symptoms.

HEIKIN JOKA –
BALANCED CLEANSING

If you have a painful right shoulder, often after you receive Reiki and it begins to feel better you may feel pain in your left shoulder. It seems that the pain has moved from the right to left but this is not the case. During the natural cleansing process your body accumulates toxins to be ejected from the system as I mentioned above. When this process takes place toxins are not collected in only one area, your body system tries to balance the toxins to help the cleansing. The process is called 'Heikin Joka' or balanced cleansing. This means that the toxins were present on both sides of the body – left and right shoulders – there was simply a little more toxin on the right side and so the pain in the left shoulder was not so apparent. Once the pain in the right side has eased that on the left side is more noticeable. This occurs in all areas of the body and it is therefore important to give Reiki to both sides equally and to explain to receivers that the process of healing or cleansing will be a gradual one.

Reiki treatment does not just heal pains or superficial symptoms, it tackles the roots or origin of the sickness. It boosts the cleansing process as it activates the immune system, the body's self-cleansing function, leading to faster and more effective cleansing without side effects.

Also as I mentioned when discussing Hayashi Sensei's seminar and the metaphor of the 'muddy stream', it is often the case that after a Reiki treatment the receiver's symptoms appear to get worse. Actually this is part of the healing and not a side effect. Toxins are hidden deep in the muscles and Reiki brings them to the surface to be removed, so it is a necessary process.

It is important for you to tell recipients of your Reiki that these things might happen and that they are positive signs so they don't need to worry unnecessarily.

五戒
GOKAI — THE FIVE PRINCIPLES

In the original Reiki, the *Gokai* — the five principles for happiness — are considered as important as *Byosen*.

Traditionally Reiki practitioners regarded these five principles as their basic philosophy of life. They chanted them once in the morning and once in the evening along with the Meiji Emperor's educational poems *(Gyosei)*. This practice distinguished Reiki practitioners from other healers.

Usui Sensei noticed that people who had overcome disease using Reiki treatment would often come back with new heath problems. He realized that if people want to be completely healthy they need to look after their psychological health along with their physical health. So he developed five principles for them to follow.

In the written principles his introduction reads, "The secret method for drawing happiness — spiritual medicine for all diseases". It recommends that Reiki practitioners chant the following words with *Gassho* style hands (hands joined together prayer style) morning and evening.

Practicing this, chant the words below three times:

Kyo dake wa	(Just for today):
Ikaru na	(Do not be angry)
Shin pai suna	(Do not be worried)
Kan sha shi te	(Be grateful)
Gyo-o hage me	(Do your duties fully)
Hito ni shin setsu ni	(Be kind to others)

Although short, these principles have deep significance. Let me explain the meaning behind them from my point of view.

Kyo dake wa / (Just for today)

The commandments of many religions tend to restrain people's thinking and make them inflexible, however anyone can decide to live well 'just for today'. This way it is possible to keep a free mind for now because the future is still open.

Life is after all just an accumulation of days, each day as important as the last or next. "I am unsure what may happen tomorrow, but I will follow the *Gokai* just for today, for this moment in time." This gradually teaches how important it is not to be trapped by yesterday and not to be anxious about tomorrow but to live in the moment and respect the 'now'.

"Kyo dake wa" is then followed by the five principles.

1ˢᵗ *principle*
Ika ru na / (Don't be angry)

Anger hurts you and others. There are many stories where just one outburst of anger leads a person into a lifetime of misery. Anger rises from many places and even when it seems justified there are often egoistic motives involved at a deeper level. Be aware of your ego and try to let it go. Self-centered people are trapped by anger, grudges and hatred and only succeed in

80

destroying themselves. Very strong anger can be soothed with Reiki. It is possible to attain an emotional and mental balance in this way.

2nd principle
Shin pai suna / (Don't be worried)

Once you are able to trust the Universe, leaving things to Universal intervention and living your life as best you can, you will be able to live in inner peace with nothing to worry about. It is difficult however to entirely discard the innate instinct to feel anxious. At least try to stop the vicious circle of worrying about being worried! If you have something bothering you, release your tension and leave the outcome to the Universe.

3rd principle
Kan sha shite / (Be grateful)

The Universe gives each of us the gift of life — without the oxygen nature provides we could not possibly survive. Once you start to appreciate the enormity of the blessings that nature provides you will be genuinely filled with pure joy. The mind clouds over with dissatisfaction however when you forget how blessed you are and become dissatisfied with what you have.

Practicing Reiki fosters thankfulness so that even when you are faced with difficulties you can look at them as possibilities and overcome them. There is nothing to be afraid of in life.

4th principle
Gyo-o hageme / (Fulfil your duties)

Gyo (duty) means not only your job but also your obligations, responsibilities and ultimately your mission in life. People can progress spiritually through their duties. Some live in seclusion to achieve this but most people learn valuable lessons and grow through everyday life and work. So this line tells you to do what you have to do and do as best as you can.

5ᵗʰ principle
Hito ni shin setsu ni / (Be kind to others)

When you help others they become willing to help other people also. Kindness is infectious. People start to help one another and, as a result, the World becomes a much better place to live in. Even if the person you have helped shows no appreciation, the wave of kindness will come back to you and you will be rewarded.

Helping others without asking for any reward from them will bring you happiness. For those who have learned Reiki, giving Reiki to others will be the best way to realize this idea.

Living your life according to these five principles will make you and others happy and healthy. You might have started Reiki primarily as a recipient because you once suffered from physical or psychological problems and needed help from others. It may have been a necessary path that you should be healed first. However don't get stuck there. First of all you must receive sufficient Reiki from others, but then thank those who have spent time giving it and the experience of healing to you. The next thing is for you to help other people in return. Ideally it is better first to be fully healed in order to heal others but it doesn't mean that a sick person cannot practice Reiki and heal other people.

Once you are to some extent healed thanks to Reiki and you have decided to live your life according to the five principles you should be ready for the next step. It is now time to help others even though you are still in the process of recovering from your own sicknesses. This step is very important for your spiritual development. The good news is that by giving Reiki to others you continue to be healed too because Reiki flows through your body before it comes out from your palms. It benefits you also. I have always encouraged even those who are ill to learn Reiki. It is a really beautiful attitude when one is willing to help others even when one is still in need.

Usui Sensei used to introduce himself as "Shin-Shin Kaizen Usui Reiki Ryo-ho Choso Usui Mikao" (Mikao Usui—founder of Usui Reiki Treatment Method of Improvement of Body and Mind). From this we can tell that he saw the human being as a unification of body and mind. It is an innovative concept that is well understood today in the ideal of holistic medicine, which sees the human as a whole. Usui Sensei was well aware of the fact that healing the physical body alone was not enough, even with Reiki, and that changing people's way of thinking was also necessary. The five principles were regarded as important for maintaining psychological health.

御製
GYOSEI—MEIJI EMPEROR'S JAPANESE STYLE WAKA POEMS

When Hayashi Sensei gave seminars he had all the participants recite *Gyosei* (Japanese style *Waka* verse[11] created by the emperors) before giving them *Reiju*. The poems were also cherished by the *Usui Reiki Ryoho Gakkai*. 'Reiki Ryoho no Shiori'—published by the organization (see Chapter 1), which mentions them clearly, saying:

"The purpose of Usui *Reiki Ryoho* is to promote in the self and in others, health and peace, hospitality and happiness throughout households, communities, nations and the whole world by developing our whole selves. We respect the messages of the *Gyosei*, created by the Meiji Emperor, along with the *Gokai* (the five principles Usui Sensei established), which help us strive to complete our life's important purpose. From the thousands of poems that the Meiji Emperor composed Usui Sensei selected 125 for us." The *Gyosei* are regarded as one of the key elements of Reiki. I was given the original *Gyosei* booklet used in Hayashi Sensei's seminar, which has 100 of 125 poems. A picture of the booklet is presented in *The Hayashi Reiki Manual*.

COMMENTARY ON THE MEIJI EMPEROR'S GYOSEI

Let me share my thoughts on ten of his verses. It seems impossible for us to translate the original atmosphere of the classical Japanese poems exactly into other languages so please forgive if the translations of the poems here don't come across as very poetic.

1.

遠くとも　人の行くべき 道ゆかば
危き事は あらじとぞ思ふ

to-o-ku-to-mo / hi-to-no-yu-ku-be-ki/ mi-chi-yu-ka-ba/
a-ya-u-ki-ko-to-wa / a-ra-ji-to-zo-o-mo-u
No matter how far you go, as long as you take the right path, nothing dangerous will come to you

No matter how unrealistic your dreams or ideals seem, you will never have to give up on them as long as you are on the path of righteousness. Don't look for the easy route, steer the necessary course. This is the surest way to realize your hopes and dreams.

2.

千早ぶる　神のひらきし 道をまた
開くは人の ちからなりけり

chi-ha-ya-bu-ru / ka-mi-no-hi-ra-ke-shi / mi-chi-o-ma-ta /
hi-ra-ku-wa-hi-to-no / chi-ka-ra-na-ri-ke-ri
On the path paved by the vigor of god, it is the vigor of people that will pave it even further.

The path paved by *kami* (god) is not always easy to pursue and it is not difficult to lose your way when you are preoccupied with trivial daily affairs. Learn from the wisdom of your predecessors. Continue making every effort to find your own way and never lose it. This applies to Reiki in that receiving *Reiju* (attunements) is not enough on its own—the most important thing is to continue to practice it.

3.

ともすれば　思はぬ方に　うつるかな
こころすべきは　こころなりけり

to-mo-su-re-ba / o-mo-wa-nu-ho-ni / u-tsu-ru-ka-na /
ko-ko-ro-su-be-ki-wa / ko-ko-ro-na-ri-ke-ri

Things are apt to go in an unexpected way.
What you have to mind is your own mind itself.

The mind wanders and it can sometimes feel out of control. However, if you take the time to observe your thoughts calmly you will find that it is not someone or something else that has created your problems, but rather it is your own mind.

In Reiki treatment there is a psychological healing treatment to help remedy psychological problems (known as *Seiheki*[13] treatment). In this way it is possible to change your thought process and stop being trapped by your ego.

4.

榊葉に　かくる鏡を　かがみにて
人もこころを　磨けとぞ思ふ

sa-ka-ki-ba-ni / ka-ku-ru-ka-ga-mi-o / ka-ga-mi-ni-te /
hi-to-mo-ko-ko-ro-o / mi-ga-ke-to-zo-o-mo-u

A divine mirror covered by the leaves of a Sakaki tree is so shiny
without any clouds.
People, polish your soul until it is as shiny as the mirror.

This poem is about a mirror covered by *Sakaki* leaves (*Sakaki* is a Japanese tree which is often used for purification at *Shinto* shrines). The mirror described is a round shaped one dedicated to a shrine. When you look at this beautifully polished mirror you will wish to have a mind that is as clear and innocent. When you pray to *kami* (god) think of this mirror and keep 'polishing' your mind.

5.

心ある 人のいさめの ことのはは
やまいなき身の　薬なりけり

ko-ko-ro-a-ru / hi-to-no-i-sa-me-no/ ko-to-no-ha-wa/
ya-ma-i-na-ki-mi-no/ ku-su-ri-na-ri-ke-ri

Disagreement of a sincere person is regarded as great preventive
medicine

Even if you think you are healthy both psychologically and
physically, achieving perfection is always difficult. It is natural
to wonder what is lacking. Therefore, when a sincere person
disagrees with you, it is best to accept what he or she says without bitterness. This is the best way to fill in a missing piece of
your life.

6.

目に見へぬ　神に向かひて　恥じざるは
人の心の まことなりけり

me-ni-mi-e-nu / ka-mi-ni-mu-ka-i-te/ ha-ji-za-ru-wa/
hi-to-no-ko-ko-ro-no / ma-ko-to-na-ri-ke-ri

Facing invisible gods without having anything to be ashamed of is
to be genuinely human.

Kami (gods) cannot be seen but exist. *Kami* must surely be aware
of our thoughts and actions in daily life. Live your life gracefully
in a way that you are not ashamed of even if *kami* is not seen.
This is the state of mind that people should possess.

7.

われもまた 更に磨かむ 曇りなき
人の心を かがみにはして

wa-re-mo-ma-ta / sa-ra-ni-mi-ga-ka-n / ku-mo-ri-na-ki
hi-to-no-ko-ko-ro-o / ka-ga-mi-ni-wa-shi-te

I (even if I am the emperor) will polish the mirror of my mind fur-
ther, learning from ordinary people who have a wonderful clarity of
mind.

There are a number of people who make a great effort to improve themselves and no matter how exalted they often remain unknown. The journey of self-discovery is not for the pursuit of fame and we should emulate this attitude when undertaking our own journey.

8.

天を恨み　人をとがむる　こともあらじ
わがあやまちを　思ふかへせば

ten-o-u-ra-mi / hi-to-o-to-ga-mu-ru / ko-to-mo-a-ra-ji
wa-ga-a-ya-ma-chi-o / o-mo-u-ka-e-se-ba

No hard feelings towards the universe or criticism of other people
would occur if we notice our own mistakes.

When someone has a run of bad luck he often blames fate or other people for his unhappiness. However if you take a moment to think about it, you will realize that blaming others for your misfortunes is not helpful — remember you have also made mistakes in the past. If you try to think of how your past mistakes have come around and created the unwanted situation you are now facing, you will stop blaming others. So, take a look at yourself before blaming others.

9.

いささかの　傷なき玉も　ともすれば
塵に光を　失ひにけり

i-sa-sa-ka-no / ki-zu-na-ki-ta-ma-mo/ to-mo-su-re-ba /
chi-ri-ni-hi-ka-ri-o / u-shi-na-i-ni-ke-ri

Even a jewel without any flaws sometimes becomes dusty and can
easily lose its sparkle.

A 'jewel without flaws', means a supremely beautiful mind. Even if your mind is in that state, the beauty will fade unless you keep improving yourself. Attaining enlightenment in itself is not enough — you need to continue making an effort to improve yourself even further.

10.

器には　従ひながら　いはがねも
とほすは水の　力なりけり

*u-tsu-wa-ni-wa / shi-ta-ga-i-na-ga-ra / i-wa-ga-ne-mo /
to-o-su-wa-mi-zu-no / chi-ka-ra-na-ri-ke-ri*

*Water is adaptable enough to allow its container to change its shape,
however it is also so powerful that it has the strength to penetrate
even a big rock.*

Water is adaptable but it is said, "Constant dripping wears away the stone". Water has great strength too. This can be applied to us — people should be flexible but also have the strength to overcome difficulties.

The ideas behind these beautiful poems are still relevant in today's world. Reading them aloud will help your mind to become purified and well balanced.

In *Jikiden Reiki* seminars we do not insist that participants recite them because we wish to respect everyone's views. However I believe that anyone who keeps these words of wisdom in mind will benefit greatly from their positive effects.

KETSUEKI KOKAN HO (KEKKO)
Blood Circulation Massage to Rejuvenate Vitality

There is another important element, which is missing in the Reiki teachings in the West today. As well as *Gokai* and *Byosen* what has also been missing is **Ketsueki Kokan Ho** (shortened name: *Kekko*) or Blood Circulation Massage. We often hear that in the West only feather touch treatments are taught and practiced, but Usui Sensei and Hayashi Sensei taught other ways of treatment using firm massage techniques such as pressing, rubbing, and patting the body of a recipient.

Reiki treatment is not only done with the hands. Other parts of the body were mentioned in the Q&A section of the *Usui Reiki Ryoho Gakkai* publication called 'Reiki Ryoho no Shiori' (Reiki Treatment Guidelines):

> Q: Does Usui *Reiki Ryoho* use any medications? Does it have any side effects?
> A: No, it doesn't use any medication or medical equipment and has no side effects. Treatment is carried out by gazing at affected areas, blowing onto them, patting, rubbing or laying hands on them.

After receiving *Reiju* anyone can radiate energy from any part of their body as well as from their hands, especially from the eyes and mouth. In some cases (such as a burn) when you cannot touch the affected area directly, it will be useful to use 'Gyo-shi' (eye-Reiki by gazing) and 'Ko-ki' (mouth-Reiki by blowing). For example with a burn, firstly you gaze at the affected area *(Gyo-shi)* and blow on it gently *(Ko-ki)* with pursed lips. Working this way in the early stages will bring much better results.

There are other methods such as rubbing *(Busyu)*, pressing *(Anju)* and patting *(Keida)*, which stimulate body fluids. The massage *Ketsueki Kokan Ho* has all these methods in it. This is essential in *Reiki Ryoho* for physical treatment. It is a great way to purify blood and rejuvenate the body. It is very effective when practiced after the ordinary hands-on physical treatment and can be practiced independently and repeatedly whenever a receiver needs it.

The sequence of the massage will be explained in detail in Chapter 5.

Chapter 4:
Japan — A Background to the Birth Place of Reiki

FIRST CONTACTS WITH NON-JAPANESE STUDENTS

I started holding *Jikiden Reiki* seminars in 1999 in Kyoto and a year later I began to give them outside of Kyoto. Now in response to requests I travel all over Japan, to Tokyo, Sapporo (in Hokkaido), Sendai (Miyagi), Kanazawa (Ishikawa), Nagoya (Aichi), Kobe (Hyogo), Takamatsu (Kagawa), Fukuoka, Kagoshima and Okinawa. I have plans to visit other places in coming years too. I do this because it's what Usui Sensei and Hayashi Sensei did. They traveled around Japan (and Hayashi Sensei even went to Hawaii) to make Reiki accessible to as many people as possible. I respect their approach and I would like to emulate it. Of course traveling back then was far more difficult than it is today and it must have called for far more patience so I can't say that I now do exactly what they used to do and I have no desire to compare myself with those great Senseis. Their level is too elevated for me to reach for anyway. I am simply trying to do the best that I can right now.

In the following year I commenced holding seminars for non-Japanese participants in Kyoto. I am still surprised that so many people from all over the world come to attend these seminars.

Since 2004 I have also started visiting other countries to give seminars. I have been to Germany, England, Hong Kong, France, Sweden, Canada and the U.S. Participants attending these seminars were not from these countries only, but also from neighboring countries. In the coming year I plan to travel to several new places, among them Portugal and Korea.

Making contact with people from spots around the world has been really intriguing. It is fascinating to learn the similarities and differences. I believe that deep down we are not really different, we just have different presentations and approaches. I would like to devote this chapter to what I have found of interest in my exchanges with non-Japanese people attending *Jikiden Reiki* seminars. Through contact with non-Japanese I have learned not only about other cultures but also about my own, although I am no cultural anthropologist. By working with these people myself I get an idea of how changes may have occurred as Reiki was passed on to the West. I see them struggle to understand things that Japanese students take for granted.

Some aspects of this chapter may not relate directly to Reiki but they may serve to give you a glimpse of Japanese culture and help you understand the background and origins of Reiki.

SEMINARS WITH PARTICIPANTS FROM OVERSEAS

From the very start of the *Jikiden Reiki* seminars with my mother we were amazed at the number of inquiries that come from overseas. We have had people from the United States, Britain, Ireland, Germany, New Zealand, Australia, Sweden, Norway, Portugal, Lithuania, Latvia, Israel, China, Canada, Netherlands, Mexico, UAE, France, Greece, Spain, Kazakhstan, Switzerland, Turkey, Russia, Korea, Taiwan, Hong Kong, Brazil, Bulgaria and more. Most of these people have already been teaching Western

Reiki and some of them are quite charismatic teachers who have thousands of students.

The content of the seminars for non-Japanese people is basically the same as for Japanese. The seminars are translated into English or other languages but we keep the original Japanese for important Reiki terms like *Gokai* and *Byosen*.

We even ask the non-Japanese participants to recite *Gokai* in Japanese because it is not only for the meaning—the sounds themselves have great spirit in them. Most visitors find this difficult but usually agree as long as they can understand what the words mean.[14]

Some Japanese *Jikiden Reiki* students are curious about what happens in these seminars for Westerners and join in as observers. These participants are usually very impressed by the numerous questions their counterparts ask. They are often ashamed to find that these Westerners are far more enthusiastic than they are. Seminars with only Japanese are much quieter—few ask questions. It's often the case that no one utters a word until I ask for questions. When there happens to be a vocal person present others will hesitantly start to open their mouths but I have had quite a few seminars with no questions asked at all.

On the other hand, in the seminars with non-Japanese, I get a barrage of questions. People are impatiently raising their hands to ask the next question while I am still answering the previous one. I do welcome questions and it is very intriguing for me to hear what is asked. I admire this aspect of Western culture very much. It turns our attention to many areas that we Japanese hardly question at all.

I also understand why non-Japanese people need to ask questions—they are trying to understand another culture, which is quite different from their own. Japanese people often don't need my explanations because what I talk in the seminar is not so difficult to understand. Anyway it is really inspiring to teach classes with non-Japanese participants. We always have great exchanges. I don't think this really means that the Japanese are less enthusiastic. A review of these different attitudes might be helpful for you to understand the Japanese culture, so I would like to include here my own idea of why we Japanese act as we do. One reason why we don't ask questions in public comes from our style of education. Japanese schools don't place importance on teaching children to have their own opinions. In most classes the teacher teaches and the students just listen to the teacher. Classes are not really interactive. Japanese are not trained to be assertive.

TRADITIONAL MASTER-DISCIPLE RELATIONSHIP

Another reason that Japanese students are rather quiet in seminars might come specifically from our traditional understanding of the 'master/disciple' relationship. In the old days in Japan students of traditional Japanese arts like say, Judo, accepted their master with almost implicit obedience. For students seeking to learn from a master, talking back or raising questions was almost unthinkable. For them their master was always right so they would accept implicitly what he said. Students were expected not to talk casually with their respected master. They always used honorific titles and acted formally towards them. There is a Japanese saying "Three steps back not to step on the master's shadow." The line was clear between a master and his students. The student learned by watching what the master did or by doing what he told them to do. So the first thing a student had to learn was acceptance and obedience. Their relationship was however quite close. They were bonded profoundly. Students looked up to their master even after they became independent and their relationship lasted throughout their whole lives, even though sometimes their status happened rise higher than that of their teacher.

The relationship between Usui Sensei and his students would not have been an exception. This would have been especially true for his prestigious students from the Navy where hierarchy was highly emphasized. I can picture them sitting up straight or standing rigidly to show great respect when they were listening to Usui Sensei. Certainly people in those days were more formal. Hayashi Sensei respected Usui Sensei so much that he would never change anything he had learned from his master even though he used his own medical knowledge to develop Reiki further. He would explain Usui Sensei's teachings in simple words for his students. Hayashi Sensei's students also had this kind of respect for their teacher. They never raised any questions about what he said. My mother and I have never had a doubt about what we learned from him, so when I get questions from my students asking why they should do this or that I sometimes don't have any other answer for them than:

"It's because this is what Hayashi Sensei said!"

In Japan today this style of relationship has pretty much disappeared but in some traditional areas it is still cherished. I am not however suggesting that my seminar participants should act in this way. I always welcome interruptions from lively students. Actually I prefer this style to the traditional Japanese style.

This tradition seems to be almost lost now but I think that most Japanese still carry the attitude unconsciously. A lot of my students are shy to ask questions because they wonder if it isn't rude. I encourage them every once in a while because I want to make sure they understand. I know they have questions because when there is someone who is brave enough to open his mouth others immediately start to ask even if most of what they ask is more practical than conceptual.

AMBIGUITY OF JAPANESE SPEECH

Another reason for this tendency might arise from the deep-rooted cultural characteristic that we are expected not to express opinions openly. Our speech is often regarded as abstract. We prefer a suggestive, often ambiguous style to a crystal clear pattern of speech. This may be because Japan is a homogeneous country and this may make it easier for us to communicate non-verbally. As an insular nation surrounded by oceans which had closed its doors to other countries for more than two centuries through the seclusion policy (from 1638 to 1853), Japan produced such a unique culture that it is difficult for non-Japanese people to comprehend. For example there is a lot of silence in our conversation and the silence is also an important part of the message. What is said verbally is not always the most important part of the message for Japanese. Sometimes what is said verbally is different from what is actually meant. One well-known example is that Japanese people use two different types of speech depending on the situation, occasion or relationship — *Honne* and *Tatemae*. *Honne* is for opinion (or action) motivated by one's true inner feelings. *Tatemae* is for an opinion (or action), which is influenced by social norms. We are required to use them separately when appropriate and to do so tactfully.

There are some situations where we find it inappropriate to say what we really mean. In Japan, which is a group-oriented society, maintaining harmony in the group is more important than the expression of individual identity. As we say in a Japanese proverb, "A nail that sticks out gets hammered down". Standing out is not always a positive thing in Japan. In order to maintain harmony we have to say what is expected and fit in with certain social situations.

We are also expected to understand the true intention when someone is using *Tatemae*. Because of this we Japanese tend to think that foreigners will understand even though we don't necessarily say things explicitly. For example, when we decline something we don't usually give a clear "No", instead we would rather say, "Let me think about it". We feel it's rude to say "No" clearly to someone's face so we will use a blurred phrase hoping the other will get the message hidden behind it. This usually works among Japanese (but it sometimes creates misunderstanding too). Keeping our true inner feeling inside in order to maintain harmony is, in a certain sense, our virtue. Of course this sometimes brings undesirable results. When in the West there is a situation where you need to become passionate in order to solve a problem you will do so even though it makes waves. The Japanese however prefer to wait until the waters are quiet. This might be seen as the principle of 'peace-at-any-price', avoiding trouble, which doesn't help solve communication gaps in this era of the global community. More open discussion is being encouraged in Japan to try to fit into this new world but it is still pitched at a low key.

This ambiguity of language has been created by these Japanese characteristics. It is one reason why it is so difficult to transmit the original ideas of Reiki, especially to the West where people place such importance on explicitness of the language. To learn and understand things that are simple but difficult to explain, like Reiki, must have been tough for the very first people who learned and taught it. The language barrier already had to be challenging enough. I say this because I hear my interpreter translating what I say to students, giving long explanations of something said in only a few words. The interpreter has to translate all the messages I give both verbally and non-verbally otherwise it would not be comprehensible. I have learned how important it is to speak clearly in the seminars to make sure the essence of Reiki is well understood. My efforts are apparently beginning to work. I have been careful even about my attitude.

My dear friend Mr. Arjava Frank Petter gave me a valuable tip. In seminars for Westerners I should look directly at participants whenever I talk to them even though I am speaking in Japanese. He knows that we Japanese usually avoid eye contact because for us it is rude to stare someone in the face. Many Japanese speakers at international conventions look at their translator instead of at the audience, which might make Westerners uncomfortable.

Participants from overseas have told me that they are happy to ask questions and find the answers they have been seeking for a long time. Those who have participated in *Jikiden Reiki* seminars are often amazed at how simple the original Reiki actually is. I myself am happily surprised that people in the West also accept and appreciate the simplicity of Reiki once they have understood it. They are even impressed with traditional Japanese culture which values 'sophisticated simplicity'. Interestingly, Japanese participants who had learned Western Reiki previously also seem to click with *Jikiden Reiki*. Some of them exclaim, "Oh, this sounds so much more like Japanese!!"

JAPANESE AND SHINTO

The Japanese today seem much more modern, and we feel we have lost our traditional cultural roots but we still have a lot of 'Japanese-ness' in us. For example in modern Japan spirituality plays a less important and more peripheral role than in the past because it has been overtaken by materialism in the last decades. Most Japanese today could be regarded as virtual atheists. Yet I believe we do still embrace traditional spirituality in every aspect of our lives even though most people today can't explain it well, if at all. Take *Shinto* (indigenous Japanese animistic religion) for example, most of us cannot describe it very well, but it exists clearly in our daily lives, in our language, food and in our views of things. People visit Shrines on auspicious days, like New Year's Day, to pay tribute to the local guardian god and to eat specially prepared food with special meanings. Shrines hold light-hearted festivals, which people enjoy very much. Lots of homes have a small *Shinto* altar. Perhaps we don't seem to take *Shinto* very seriously today because it is something we take for granted and don't think about, as the same way we don't think about the parts of our bodies.

I believe understanding *Shinto* is beneficial for those who learn Reiki because it is the ancient spiritual root of Japanese culture. So it is quite natural that Usui Sensei would have used a lot of ideas based in *Shinto*. I would like to explain this here based on what I have learned in my own study of *Shinto* and from information gathered from books and other sources. To explain *Shinto* thoroughly would be quite impossible because of its vastness and its simplicity. What I am writing here is quite basic in the hope that it will help those who don't know *Shinto* very well. For the further information please refer to books on *Shinto*.

WHAT IS SHINTO?

Shinto is the earliest and most distinctive of the Japanese religions. Today's *Shinto* was developed from our primitive animistic worship of natural phenomena — the sun, mountains, trees, water, rocks, our harvest and so on. Animism embraces the idea that spirits inhabit all of creation and look after us human beings. It was generated naturally by ancient people in prehistoric Japan who were awe struck by the greatness of nature, so it doesn't have a particular founder and it has never had any doctrines or scriptures. *Shinto* doesn't have any missionaries as other religions do, nor is it very assertive. I think this is intrinsically connected to what I was saying earlier about our cultural characteristics, that we Japanese are not assertive.

Shinto was generated with a notion of *kami* or deities and started in the form of rituals and ceremonies, which makes *Shinto* unique. *Kami* in *Shinto* is different from God in the Christian sense. *Kami* is something divine, or it can be translated as the divine energy existing in everything in nature, so *kami* can be anything. Even people can be *kami* because no line was drawn between man and nature. Ancestors are also worshipped because our life and our soul would not have been given without them. The ancestors' lives were, in turn, given by their ancestors. We are here thanks to them and also thanks to all the *kami* of Mother Nature. *Shinto* sees everything, including human beings, as linked to the source or the divine world. Its rituals are not meant to be carried out for salvation, so its prayers are not like other religious prayers. They are prayers of gratitude in advance for future blessings and devoted commitments to ones duties. Original *Shinto* rituals started in order to tell the *kami* of successfully completed tasks, such as the rice harvest, and to thank them for their invisible helping hand. *Shinto's* basic idea is for you to do your best and leave the outcome to universal intention.

Before Buddhism was introduced Japan was a land blessed with *Shinto*. In those ancient times in Japan *Shinto* was not initially seen as a religion. They did not even have a name for it. It was called *Shinto* by those who brought Buddhism to Japan around the 6th century. They saw many people carrying out mysterious rituals by the sea, in the mountains and at the rivers and they became curious. They were told that they were practicing 'the way of kami' and hence the name *Shinto* which means 'the Kami Way'.

Later *Shinto* was manipulated by the government and used to create nationalism during the 19th century, which drove Japan into militarism. 'State Shinto' was created to force people to worship the imperial lineage. And actually this lineage was originally related very closely to ancient *Shinto* and from the previous century until the end of World War II the government used this to create patriotism in the people. It was far removed from the very friendly and peaceful essence of *Shinto*.

There are still a lot of beautiful *Shinto* shrines all over Japan where sophisticated and symbolic rituals are still practiced. In Kyoto where I live countless shrines are still cherished and visited by many people. *Shinto* shrines are not built with the same idea as Buddhist temples. Let me tell you briefly how these *Shinto* shrines started.

As I have said *Shinto* started as a primitive animistic worship of natural phenomena. Ancient people living harmoniously with nature were filled with awe. They would feel energized when near a certain natural object or place. For example people might notice that they felt good being near or touching a specific tree on some mountain. Finding healing energy there they would mark

Tree with Shimenawa (on Mount Kurama)

it as a sacred tree to distinguish it from others by tying a holy rope around it. This was the origin of today's *Shimenawa*.

In other places where folk experienced divine energy coming from a certain power spot on a mountain they would build a fence around it. They designated the space inside the fence as sacred and created an entry gate. This gate is the origin of the *Torii Gate*, which you find at the entrance of *Shinto* shrines everywhere today. In yet other regions there were other objects of worship, typically a big rock or a powerful waterfall. Later in these kinds of places a small house was built for those who guarded the sanctuary. They lived there not only to protect the sanctuary but to serve as oracles to deliver messages from the divine or as healers who could help the sick. In this way *Shinto* shrines developed into places where people lived and performed rituals. And even today you can still feel the good energy when you visit these shrines.

The interesting thing about animistic *Shinto* is that spirits inhabit not only objects and places in nature but everything

Torii Gate in Ise shrine.

everywhere, including inanimate objects in a house such as an oven in the kitchen, a well and even the bathroom. Spirits, which we call *Kotodama*, also occupy the intangible, like the words we speak and write.

KOTODAMA

As I mentioned previously the Japanese language is ambiguous and doesn't state opinions or ideas very clearly so, although it may sound a little contradictory, from ancient times the Japanese have cherished words. In Japan we believe that words have energy, which we call *Kotodama*. (Word Spirit)

Kotodama is a miraculous power, which inhabits words and controls our fortune and misfortune depending on how the words are used. This was believed emphatically in ancient Japan and even now Japanese people unconsciously embrace it. For example when someone says that something might go wrong, others will say, "Don't say such an ominous thing! What if this should make it really happen?" We have some words which by tacit agreement should not be used in certain circumstances. For example we are told not to use words like 'break', 'end' or 'cut' at wedding ceremonies, so when a guest is winding up the congratulatory speech for a newly married couple he would conclude by saying, "I will knot my words", rather than, "I will end my words." Clearly we still believe that we manifest situations through the power of the words we use. Our ancestors used *Kotodama* power purposefully to change the surrounding environment or an event. Because of this understanding ancient Japanese were careful not to speak recklessly. This also may have had its influence on the ambiguity of our language.

Japanese today are often criticized by Western people for not giving clear opinions and instead showing a rather strange smile. It must be confusing and it is very difficult for them to know what their Japanese counterpart is thinking. One reason for this tendency (there may be others) comes from our unconscious habit of being very careful about what we say. This has on occasion been the cause of miscommunication in contemporary global politics. Yet cherishing words to this extent creates a beautiful spiritual climate and I have heard it said that Japanese is one of the cleanest languages in the world. We don't have many swear words and I rejoice in the recent tendency here to revive the culture of treasuring beautiful words. Today books on beautiful words make the best-seller lists.

PROVING KOTODAMA ENERGY – MEETING MR. MASARU EMOTO

Words have energy. Good words have good vibrations and give great energy. I always wanted to prove that such invisible energy exists but I did not know how to make visible the invisible. So I was delighted when Mr. Masaru Emoto found a way to do it. His innovative idea of crystallizing water made it possible to show how words affect water. Mr. Emoto said beautiful words such as "Ai" (love) or "Arigato" (thank you) to a sample of water and froze it at a certain temperature to form a crystal of ice. Beautiful words create beautifully shaped crystals. Ugly words create an ugly shape or no shape at all. So even though the original water is taken from a tap in a big city, which is not very natural and will not make crystalline shapes as it is, giving beautiful words to it will change its quality for the better and produce beautiful, harmonious shaped crystals.

Mr. Emoto and his group first undertook this experiment to see if music might have an impact on water. They discovered that water makes beautiful crystals when played beautiful music. Spontaneously came the interesting idea that words may have similar effect. It was a great success. Thanks to their endeavor now with our own eyes we can see reflected the intangible energy of words.

Mr. Masaru Emoto says in his wonderful book, 'The Hidden Messages in Water',

> *"The result of the experiments didn't disappoint us. Water exposed to **Thank you** formed beautiful hexagonal crystals, but water exposed to the word **Fool** produced crystals similar to water exposed to heavy-metal music, malformed and fragmented.... The lesson that we can learn from this experiment has to do with the power of words. The vibration of good words has a positive effect on our world, whereas the vibration from negative words has the power to destroy".*

He notes that 70% of our body is made up of water so the vibrations of words will affect the water circulating inside us. It becomes vitally important to use good words toward yourself and others.

In recent years Mr. Emoto's books have become very popular in the West especially in Switzerland. I had great respect for him even before he became such a famous figure. When I read his first book on Hado (wave fluctuation, vibration) in 1992 I was thrilled to discover that we could now finally prove the existence of invisible energies. In quantum mechanics everything is described as being made up of the vibration of molecules. The human body, human thought, emotions are also transmitted via vibrations, which we call Hado in Japanese. What really impressed me was his discovery that sicknesses commence from a distortion of *Hado.*

This distortion must be what in Reiki we call *Byosen.* Mr. Emoto started using water to repair distortions by copying positive information to the water and having the ill person drink it for healing. In Reiki we find *Byosen* with our hands and

105

direct Reiki energy to that area. We use different methods but the basic theory is the same.

I was so fascinated with his ideas that I took a teacher's license with IHM (International Hado Membership), Mr. Emoto's organization, and studied his work. I invited him to talk to *Jikiden Reiki* students in Tokyo and Kyoto in 2004 and my dream of being able to physically demonstrate Reiki energy came true in the form of his water crystals. I asked the organization to examine water that had been exposed to Reiki. I am showing them here for your reference.

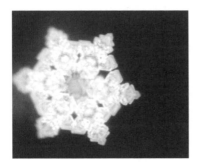 

Left: Water with the kotodama 'Seiheki'.
Right: Water given Jikiden Reiki (ihm051109014)

I am afraid that these explanations of Mr. Emoto's ideas may not be very accurate so I strongly recommend that to gain an appreciation of his wonderful work you read his books yourself. They have been translated into several languages so I hope you can find them easily. When you see the photos of the beautiful crystals generated by the loving energy of spoken words I am sure that, like me, you will be stimulated to use positive words only. All the time.

SHINTO AND KOTODAMA IN REIKI

GOKAI FOR THE PURIFICATION
OF A VENUE WITH ITS KOTODAMA

Kotodama inhabits Reiki, for example, in *Gokai*. As I indicated following *Gokai* (the five principles) is vital for us Reiki practitioners. The five principles are important for maintaining psychological health and as a result we will also enjoy physical health.

The teachings of the *Gokai* were not all originated by Usui Sensei himself. He selected useful lines from various teachings and compiled them. Within the words of the *Gokai, Kotodama* is alive because these words were chosen very carefully by a grand teacher, Usui Sensei himself.

Prior to each *Reiju* (attunement) Hayashi Sensei always had the participants in his seminars recite the *Gokai* with him. Through this reciting the venue was purified by the enormous power and the attunements were ready.

We still practice this same *Gokai* at our *Jikiden Reiki* seminars today. The sounds of the words contain the great energy of *Kotodama* and we even ask non-Japanese participants to recite them in the original Japanese. I always use the scroll which has the *Gokai* written on it. The calligraphy is actually a replica of the original drawn by Hayashi Sensei. In the old days Hayashi Sensei instructed all the *Shihans* to hang the scroll in the venue whenever they practiced *Reiju*. In *Jikiden Reiki* I ask *Shihan* students to do the same when they teach. Because of the splendid wording put together by Usui Sensei and the sophisticated calligraphy of Hayashi Sensei the scroll pulses with magnificent energy. Some students have said that they can see bright light radiating from it in the dark. It actually changes the atmosphere in a room

The scroll is sold at *Jikiden Reiki* institute. I used the word 'sell' but it is not the best word to use here. This scroll is not available to everyone. Students have to wait until they become *Shihan-kaku* for permission to purchase it. In the old days my family considered it a great honor to have obtained the scroll from Hayashi Sensei. We keep a register of people who own one.

KAMIZA AND SHIMOZA — THE ENERGY FLOW IN A ROOM

We have to choose the location for the scroll carefully. In a room the *ki* (*qi* in Chinese), or energy, flows in a certain direction. For the scroll we need to find the highest energy spot in the room (*Kamiza*) since energy usually flows from up to down like a river. *Kamiza* is the higher energy and *Shimoza* is the lower. This *Shinto*-related concept is regularly seen in everyday situations like company conferences. There is a certain rule as to who sits where. Usually the most senior person present sits in the *Kamiza* to make sure the conference goes as smoothly as possible. It is especially efficient to use this understanding of the flow of energy when we work with such energy as Reiki. So we put the scroll in the *Kamiza* and the teacher in the seminar stands right there.

HOW THEN DO WE FIND THE KAMIZA?

It is easy to find the *Kamiza* in a Japanese room. You usually find a recess or alcove called a *Tokonoma* in a traditional Japanese room and this determines the *Kamiza* spot. Most often it is installed in the farthest corner from the entrance. There you usually find a scroll with a picture or calligraphy, which has been selected to suit the season or the occasion. The *Gokai* scroll can easily fit there.

When you have a seminar in a Western style room however you have to find the location for a *Tokonoma*. As we have seen, the highest energy spot in a room is likely to be in the farthest corner from the entrance, it works the same way even in a Western room. So this is where we hang the scroll. The area needs to be kept clean and tidy.

Whenever I hold a seminar in a hotel or convention room away from Kyoto I choose the place for the scroll this way.

This should also be considered when we give a treatment. Whenever possible the practitioner should work in the highest energy spot in the treatment room. Position the receiver's head so it is pointing toward the *Kamiza* because energy flows into the body from the head. You, as the practitioner, start out by sitting next to the *Kamiza* to give Reiki to the recipient's head. (From there you can move to lay your hands on other parts of the body).

I often discuss this in seminars and a surprising number of Western participants find it really interesting.

Tokonoma

KOTODAMA AND GYOSEI

Kotodama clearly resides in the *Gyosei*, the Meiji emperor's *Waka* poems, which Usui Sensei encouraged his students to recite. For the average Japanese the emperors are an indispensable aspect of their identity. I would like to explain a little bit more about the background of the Meiji Emperor's *Gyosei*. This Japanese style of poetry demonstrates how we cherish simplicity. *Waka* and *Haiku* (another style of Japanese poem) are constructed of few words and leave the interpretation of the meaning to the reader. There is more about *Gyosei* in Chapter 3.

THE MEIJI EMPEROR

It is often said that the Meiji Emperor (who reigned from 1868 to 1912) radiated a richer air of nobility than any other emperor in Japanese history. He was a very open, inspiring man with a strong sense of charity and was receptive to new ideas yet consistent in his beliefs.

The chief retainers at the forefront of politics at the time were impressive leading figures who had endured and overcome the upheavals during the transitional period between the last days of the Tokugawa Shogunate[15] (1603-1867) and the modernization period of the Meiji Restoration[16] in the late 19th century. Yet the Meiji Emperor was said to emit such a penetrating energy that even these great men couldn't meet him without perspiring. It is easy to imagine just how great the authority of the emperors was for Japanese people in those days. However, recognition of the Meiji Emperor's great qualities extended beyond the boundaries of Japan. The then President of America, Franklin Roosevelt, came to visit the Meiji Emperor and spoke with him in person. President Roosevelt's comment on his impression of the Emperor was: "The Meiji Emperor's incredible personality is incomparable to any other leader of any place or time in history.

110

He is the greatest emperor and Japan is very fortunate to have him. Under his care they will be led to a prosperity that others would never be able to achieve."

President Roosevelt may have said this out of a desire to be courteous, however it was quite exceptional for a head of state to praise another in this way. It could be said that the President was so impressed by the Emperor that he momentarily forgot his own position in giving such an incredible compliment.

The Meiji Emperor was known as a quiet person who expressed his inner feelings through his poems. A talented literary man, he composed over 100,000 poems in the course of his life. If he produced ten a day it would have taken a little over 27 years to complete. His poems have been highly acclaimed as both educational and cultural assets of Japan. Usui Sensei so greatly admired the Meiji Emperor's personal grace and his many virtues that he selected his most outstanding poems as guidelines for spiritual enhancement.

Japan's current Emperor or *Tenno*, Akihito, is the 3rd generation after the Meiji Emperor. When the current Emperor Akihito's father, Emperor Hirohito (the Showa Emperor), issued a statement renouncing his own divinity after Japan had lost World War II, he also renounced sovereign power. The post war constitution of 1947 defined the emperor as 'the symbol of the State and the unity of the people' rather than the ruler of the country. Today the imperial family is still respected by Japanese people but this is now more a question of affection than of power. The current Emperor and Empress are both loved by the people for their caring and warm personalities. Japan's younger generation however is quite indifferent toward them. We have now a completely different situation from the time of the Meiji Emperor.

SHINTO INFLUENCED BY BUDDHISM

In the 6th century (said to be in 538), Buddhism was introduced into Japan from India via China and Korea and has had a broad influence on Japanese culture. *Shinto* also was greatly affected by Buddhism, but having a polytheistic nature with its 'Yao-yorozu no kami' or 8 million gods it has served to create a fuzzy picture of religion in Japan. Even today the Japanese are not so particular about having a certain belief. A lot of people claim to be Buddhist but most of them don't have clear Buddhist identity.

In Japan many people visit a *Shinto* shrine when a baby is born, get married at a Christian church even if they are not Christian at all (a lot of the younger generation prefer a western style wedding), and conduct the funeral at a Buddhist temple. It must seem very inconsistent to non-Japanese people but we don't really find it inconsistent. From this perspective it should not have been so difficult for the ancient Japanese to accept the newly imported Buddhism.

Buddhism and *Shinto* co-existed quite naturally, with *Shinto* shrines becoming guardians and links for Buddhist monasteries. That is why, when you visit a temple in Japan, you can often find a *Shinto* shrine inside. *Shinto* has mostly transformed itself quite flexibly and naturally although some practitioners could not adapt to the changes and were driven into the mountains to practice ancient *Shinto* in its pure form. There is now a quiet movement to restore this original *Shinto*.

ZEN BUDDHISM

I would like to mention another important factor in understanding the Japanese — *Zen* spirit. I am not, however, going into details of *Zen* because I believe many readers are more knowledgeable about it than I am. So I will just say a little about how *Zen* has affected the outlook in Japan in the hope that it will help you grasp another aspect of Japanese spiritual culture.

Zen was brought to Japan from China and evolved here into today's version of Japanese *Zen*. (I have heard that what the Chinese knew as *Zen* was already very different from the original Indian Buddhism.) For further information there are many good books on *Zen* such as 'Zen and Japanese culture' by Daisetz T. Suzuki.

At the end of the 12th century a *Zen* Buddhist sect was established in Japan and the spirit of *Zen* deeply influenced the Japanese character. The ultimate purpose of *Zen* is the same as original Buddhism — to gain freedom from suffering and to free all those who suffer.

A key characteristic of *Zen* Buddhism is its aim to achieve spiritual enlightenment (or Satori) through the practice of 'Zazen' or sitting meditation. It emphasizes self-control, which appealed to the Samurai (or warrior) class and their code of ethics some centuries ago. Our respected Usui Sensei studied at a *Zen* temple for three years in search of enlightenment, *An-Jin-Ryu-Mei* or the state of complete stillness.

Zen nourished many branches of the arts in Japan as it did in China. Here, beautiful arts flourished such as *Shodo* (Japanese calligraphy), *Kado* (flower arrangement), *Kyudo* (archery), *Sado* (tea ceremony), *Koudo* (incense ceremony), and many others. These arts were developed to help people concentrate, to become one pointed and enter the state of no mind, which is not disturbed by a busy conscious mind. *Zen* contributed to the building of our particular taste for beauty, which appreciates 'sophisticated simplicity' and silence.

It is unfortunate that many Japanese today seem to be indifferent toward these beautiful aspects of our tradition, cherished and handed down to us by our ancestors. Foreign visitors to Japan seeking this spiritual quality must be disappointed at this recent trend. In fact our visitors often understand and appreciate traditional Japanese cultural assets far better than we do ourselves.

TODAY'S JAPANESE AND REIKI

Not only *Shinto* and Buddhism, but other religions such as esoteric Buddhism, Confucianism and even Christianity have had their influence on our Japanese spiritual heritage. I am not knowledgeable enough to discuss these but what I can say here is that we have adapted to new ideas quite flexibly and change them easily to suit our own taste. Some imported influences have gone through a great process of development and flourished more than in their birthplace. We Japanese have a tendency to appreciate new ideas introduced from foreign countries and I do wonder if this is not the case with Reiki.

Reiki originated in Japan but faded into silence only to regain popularity after being reintroduced from the West. I suspect that it might have been very difficult for Reiki to revive here without traveling through this channel. A lot of Japanese people have begun to wonder about Reiki simply because they hear that it's popular in the West. "Hmmm, the word Reiki sounds Japanese, but I have never heard of it. What is it?" Quite a few Japanese people have come to us this way. The funny thing is that they will buy something Japanese only when they find that non-Japanese people appreciate it. If Reiki had not been reintroduced from overseas modern Japan might have completely ignored it as some outdated thing from the past. So I strongly believe that this has been a necessary path for Reiki to travel.

In any case Reiki has traveled around the globe radiating great energy. It has been welcomed and cherished everywhere around the world and now is being welcomed home. During the trip it absorbed a variety of beautiful spiritual assets. Now it needs to reabsorb the original Japanese simplicity and bring this to the people of the world in return. I also hope that the Japanese, by learning Reiki, will honor our traditional culture and respect the invisible spirits that bless us. I am certain that Reiki will continue to serve as a bridge connecting people to people and people to the universe.

REIKI OR 靈氣

The word 'Reiki' is spread all over the World today. Even the authoritative "Collins English Dictionary" introduced it with the definition — 'type of spiritual therapy'. "The Gale Encyclopedia of Alternative Medicine" in the US includes the word with a favorable comment, saying "Reiki — a touch therapy used in much the same way to achieve similar effects that traditional massage therapy is used — to relieve stress and pain and to improve the symptoms of various health conditions."

Originally the word Reiki is written as 靈氣 in Japanese *Kanji* characters. (*Kanji* are one of the Japanese writing styles coming from China. *Kanji* all have a meaning. The others are just phonetic letters.)

Here the word Reiki is often written in phonetic letters as if it was a foreign word even though it originated in Japan because most of the Reiki spreading here today is the one reintroduced from the West.

Another reason why we tend to avoid using the original *Kanji* is that the character 靈 (Rei) has a connotation of something freaky like a ghost. This happens because a lot of people misunderstand the true meaning of the word. Some cult groups have used this character in their names, so many Japanese people when they hear the word take Reiki to be associated with one of those.

Kanji characters are pictographs and ideograms. The *Kanji* 靈 (Rei) has a profound meaning in itself. Beyond the meaning 'spirit of the dead', the word actually connotes 'a soul', 'a god', 'divine being', 'sanctity', 'awesomeness', or 'mercy'. Thus the word Reiki indicates a divine energy, which is the highest of all solar energies.

When we analyze it more closely we can also find an interesting message. The character 靈 is divided into parts and each part has its meaning. The top part of the character 靈consists of 雨 and 口口口. The topmost,雨, means rainfall. The ancient Chinese knew that rain was indispensable for agriculture so it was regarded as a blessing from the universe. In the lower part you will find '口口口'. Each square-looking character signifies a mouth or a container (utsuwa—器 a body with mouths). So the top two parts symbolize receiving divine energy into our body (as a container) through our mouths. The bottom part, 巫, indicates a medium, someone who serves the gods and brings us messages from the divine.

So the character 靈 carries a significant message. Altogether it means that human beings possess the ability to connect with the divine to receive beneficial energy (via a medium), which works wonderfully not only on physical symptoms but also on the spiritual plane.

The other part of the character, 氣 (ki), has been simplified in today's Japanese to 気. When you compare the two you will find a slight difference in the bottom parts. The former has 米 in it whereas the new letter has メ.

This difference is very significant and it is preferable to stick to the old character, which has 米 because its shape shows the radiation of energy. The meaning of the character itself is important as well. The letter 米 means rice, which is a source of energy especially in Asian countries. The one with 乂 indicates X or 'ending or stopping the energy flow'.

You might say this is just a word game but we believe that the choice of words is very important because, as we have seen, words have energy. Our ancestors formed them with 'Koto-dama', great spirits. We wish to respect them so we do not want them changed.

SOME NOTES ON THE JAPANESE WRITING SYSTEM

KANJI, HIRAGANA, AND KATAKANA

Written Japanese is a blend of three writing styles. The first and main one is *Kanji* (ideographs originally imported from China). Each *Kanji* letter is a symbol for a concept and is used for writing content words or root elements with other parts supplemented by Hiragana — or Japanese phonetic symbols. The second is *Hiragana*, a phonetic alphabet that was developed in the 9th century as an efficient way to write Japanese. It supplements the gaps created by the difference between the languages (Chinese and Japanese). It is derived from the shape of the Chinese characters. It also serves as a stepping-stone for elementary school children before they learn the more complex *Kanji*. The third is *Katakana*, which is also a phonetic alphabet used nowadays mainly to indicate foreign words. Since the 1980's the word Reiki has often been seen written in *Katakana* in magazines and in advertisements of Japanese who practice Western Reiki suggesting that it is something foreign.

AN ENGLISH WOMAN IN KYOTO

BY AMANDA JAYNE

A CULTURAL PERSPECTIVE –
MY EXPERIENCE IN JAPAN

When I first came to Japan I naively thought that I would fully understand Japanese culture in about 6 months. This did not happen. Now, almost five years later, I can honestly say that I still do not understand Japanese culture. What I have found though, is that it is easy to fall in love with the culture precisely because it is so multi-layered and has an incredible depth to it – a depth that many Japanese people tell me they do not understand either. I think the depth can be very deceptive too. Looking at the surface of young Japanese society today it is easy to believe that there is little of the former culture and tradition remaining. However beneath this surface lie layers of the older culture interwoven into daily life and beliefs in general. I think of it like a thick woven tapestry in which new strands have been added onto the surface but which are also interwoven with the old such that they are inextricably linked, even though from the top it may sometimes appear that there is more of the new than the old.

Some people here are living on the surface and do not wish to look into the layers underneath. Yet some actively study the more traditional aspects of the culture such as the tea ceremony (sado), calligraphy (shodo) or Japanese flower arranging (Ikebana or Sado) to name only a few. My first experience of these traditions left me wondering how something with apparently so little to it could possibly be so deeply ingrained in a culture. When I tried the Tea ceremony for example, I found myself sitting in silence in a wooden teahouse on tatami mats for a very long time. Several women wearing beautiful kimonos undertook a very simple but lengthy ritual of making tea using specific utensils, which they showed to each person in the room before using them. Within ten minutes I was squirming around on my cushion looking for something in the room to soak up my attention. There was nothing but a *kanji* character in calligraphy on the wall, one flower and the paper screen doors around us. It seemed like a very long time before we got to drink our tea.

Over the last couple of years however I have come to appreciate that the majority of Japanese people seem to have an inherent appreciation for the exquisite beauty that can be seen in the simplest of things, if only one takes the time to sit and be with it. I can see now that the tea ceremony is not so much about having a cup of tea (my original idea) but more about this appreciation of the beauty in all things, from the utensils to the calligraphy on the wall, to the silence and atmosphere in the room—and even the movements made by the servers. I am well aware that I still may not have really grasped everything behind it but this is where I am at the moment and it explains more about other aspects of the culture for me too.

Although, as I said, some people are living in the newer, top layers of the tapestry, I notice that the influence of the deeper layers is still present in everyday life. I guess in the same way that the shrines and temples lie close to or sometimes amongst the designer stores and high street shops in Kyoto, many of the spiritual concepts of ancient *Shinto* and the religious concepts of Buddhism are an integral part of language and society. When I have asked people here if they are followers of Buddhism or *Shinto*, I have often been told that whilst some people are Buddhists, it is impossible not to be *Shinto* as it is not a religion so much as a true appreciation and respect for the God or 'kami' energy in everything, particularly nature and all those who have gone before us. Some people seem to see it as a part of being Japanese. I used to be very confused about the nature of and connection between *Shinto* and Japanese Buddhism in Japan today — and having read about them I can safely say that I am still confused. As with so many other parts of Japanese culture now, though the distinction may seem obvious at first, as soon as you peel back the layers there are crossings over and links that make it difficult to define where one ends and the other begins. What is clear however, is that once again, in both of these philosophies, the concepts of simplicity and beauty within all things is present.

The difference between the elaborate and decorative Buddhist temples and the plain, simple Japanese ones is a clear indication of the lack of need for beauty on the outside to avoid compromising the beauty inherent in simplicity.

Simplicity is key in *Jikiden Reiki*. Looking at and understanding the meaning behind the few symbols and *kanji* used is something I believe to be very important and has helped me to understand some of the incredible depths lying beneath the simplicity. The five principles that Usui Sensei originally devised were very simple too. At some seminars I have talked to people who feel either that they are not really a necessary part of Reiki or that they are too direct. I also felt this way but my ideas gradually changed and now looking at what lies behind each concept I realize that in these five short sentences is wisdom that really can make a difference to life and health. The changes that I sometimes see in these are another example of adding to the outside of things rather than looking at what is on the inside.

To my mind *Jikiden Reiki* and the concepts woven into Japanese culture that I have talked about are conspicuously linked and I feel that, as a non-Japanese, it has taken me a long time to appreciate the incredible depth that is part of such a simple thing. When I look at how Reiki has changed around the World, I can't help but wonder if it is because non-Japanese cultures find it difficult to grasp the idea that everything you need is within you already and is so simple. Much has been added to the original teachings of Reiki and although it may be very effective and could never be called 'wrong' in any way, I can't help but feel that the need always to add things on the outside takes us away from appreciating and experiencing the depths — the raw power and beauty of what is already there.

Chapter 5:
Practical Application

RYOHO SHISHIN (TREATMENT INSTRUCTION MANUAL)

By Hayashi Reiki Kenkyukai

WHAT IS RYOHO SHISHIN?

Here I would like to introduce a manual called *Ryoho Shishin* (Treatment Manual) published by the *Hayashi Reiki Kenkyukai*. It is a very simple manual, which gives Reiki practitioners guidelines on treatments according to clients' symptoms and diseases.

This is a partial introduction really. In the future I am planning to write a full book commenting on this treatment guide. For detailed information please refer to my earlier publication 'The Hayashi Reiki manual', written together with Frank Arjava Petter.

Ryoho Shishin (Treatment Guide)

Head in general (head, brain disease, headaches)

1) forehead 2) temples 3) back of the head and neck 4) crown

*Treatments to the head should be done for all ailments. When there is a headache spend a lot of time on the aching area.

- **The flu**

  1) nose 2) throat 3) trachea 4) bronchus 5) lungs 6) liver 7) pancreas 8) stomach 9) intestines 10) kidneys 11) head 12) *Kekko Massage*

- **Anemia, leukemia, scurvy**

  1) heart 2) liver 3) pancreas 4) stomach 5) intestines 6) kidneys 7) spinal column 8) *Kekko Massage*

- **Diabetes**

  1) liver 2) pancreas 3) heart 4) stomach 5) intestines 6) bladder 7) kidneys 8) head 9) spinal column 10) *Kekko Massage*

Here you can find the names of the organs to be treated for each disease and symptom but it does not indicate that practitioners should follow a certain order when they lay their hands to give Reiki treatments.

This guidebook gives some hints for when you cannot find the *Byosen* by yourself — by laying hands on the suggested areas until you do find *Byosen*. When you find an affected area give Reiki intensively until the sensation eases. Tackle all the *Byosen* this way and after you have dealt with them all finish the treatment with the *Kekko Massage.*

Intuition which arises with experience is helpful in finding the *Byosen,* the causes of disease. However, even for a beginner, once the hands can sense *Byosen* a little bit anybody can give effective treatments with the guidance of the manual.

BASIC RULES FOR REIKI TREATMENT

As suggested in the *Ryoho Shishin* the head is the most important part so we always treat that regardless of the symptoms. It is because of the basic nature of Reiki, 'flowing from the top to the bottom', that we begin a treatment by laying our hands on the head. Reiki then flows through the whole body. On its way it moves to each part of the body and stops wherever there is disease or blockages to the flow. It is the blockages, which cause disease. Reiki works on these regions and enables them to regain their original functions.

Thus it is always necessary for the practitioner to treat the head of the recipient starting with the forehead, moving to the back of the head and then both temples and the crown. When finding a strong *Byosen* in any of these four places concentrate there. People today frequently suffer from excessive stress so most have *Byosen* in at least one position on the head.

When there are two practitioners one can concentrate on the head area and the other on the diseased region. When there are three practitioners the extra person lays their hands on the soles of the feet, which, next to the head, are the most important areas. From the Oriental Medical perspective the soles of the feet contain a map of the meridian points. When laying hands on them we can actually feel the flow of *ki* (or *qi* in Chinese) circulating in the body. The soles of the feet give us a lot of information about the state of health. When they get warmer it means the blood circulation in the body is improved. For someone with poor circulation it often takes 20 minutes for the soles to warm up. If the circulation is seriously poor give at least a full hour. Even though it may take a long time to deal with a problem Reiki is very effective and its effect lasts because it is not external. It warms the body from the inside. People don't take poor blood circulation seriously enough, yet when it is treated and returned to normal their list of ailments will be greatly reduced.

In addition Hayashi Sensei's *Ryoho Shishin* states that the soles of the feet are very effective points at which to give Reiki when there is a problem in the mouth. Usui Sensei's *Ryoho Shishin* does not mention this, so I believe that it must be Hayashi Sensei's discovery.

HOW BYOSEN SPREADS IN THE BODY

In the center of the sole of the foot there is an initial meridian point leading to the kidney. When a practitioner lays hands on this part of both soles the receiver can actually feel Reiki flowing to the kidneys, which are very important organs.

As I mentioned in Chapter 3 it is often the case that illness begins with a blockage generated in the region of the kidneys. Most everyday backaches that many Japanese people complain about actually come from their malfunctioning kidneys. When the important function of filtering the blood is not working well organs can't release the toxins, which accumulate around them.

These toxins migrate to between the shoulder blades creating *Byosen* there and spread further up to the shoulders and around the armpits. From the shoulders *Byosen* often continues to spread to the neck and even up the back of the head (medulla oblongata). If the *Byosen* there is strong it is an early warning indicating the risk of a stroke.

When *Byosen* is scattered all over the body — the back, the shoulders and the neck, at least three treatments are needed for them to clear. In the old days practitioners were encouraged to give Reiki around the receiver's shoulders and neck in the first treatment, then to the head in the second session and to the kidneys in the third. When you find a strong *Byosen*, concentrate on this area.

A TREATMENT EXAMPLE
(Treatment for the Flu)

Let me take the flu as an example to show how to give a detailed treatment using *Ryoho Shishin.*

- **The flu**
  1) nose 2) throat 3) trachea 4) bronchus 5) lungs 6) liver 7) pancreas 8) stomach 9) intestines 10) kidneys 11) head 12) *Kekko Massage*

The main purpose of a Reiki treatment in a case of flu is to improve the flow of *ki* (*qi*) and blood circulation in the upper body. By consulting the teaching manual for suggestions as to where to lay the hands to detect sensations, practitioners can find *Byosen* in at least one of these regions. It means the area needs intensive Reiki.

After you have dealt with all the *Byosen* in the body it is time for the *Kekko Massage* to finish off the treatment. This stimulates the blood circulation and renders the hands on treatment even more effective. The blood in the body flows more smoothly and the whole body becomes warmer resulting in an alleviation of the ailments.

DIFFERENCES BETWEEN TWO RYOHO SHISHIN

As you might know the *Usui Reiki Ryoho Gakkai* also published their *Ryoho Shishin.* Their manual was put together by Usui Sensei and it is different from the one published by the *Hayashi Reiki Kenkyukai.*

Usui Sensei placed importance on symptoms caused by distortions of the spine, therefore in his manual he mentions the various spinal vertebrae by name, for instance 'T-2' (2nd vertebra of the thoracic vertebrae). Chiropractic theory was first introduced to Japan around the time Usui Sensei was teaching Reiki, so he may have been inspired and adapted its concepts.

On the other hand, Hayashi Sensei's *Ryoho Shishin* focuses more on organs and doesn't mention any individual vertebrae. Hayashi Sensei's manual is based on a medical practitioner's point of view.

I am not suggesting that either is right or wrong. They wrote their manuals from different points of view. They had different backgrounds. Both of the manuals were provided to give guidelines on where to find the *Byosen*, so the differences are only in their expression.

KETSUEKI KOKAN HO (KEKKO) — THE MASSAGE AND ITS PROCEDURE

The massage follows a certain sequence.[17]

Have the receiver lie down face down. It is better they wear light clothing.

1. Find the indentations located either side of the neck at the base of the skull (C2 area). Place your thumb and index finger there, and draw with your fingers a symbol (the first symbol taught in our seminar. The symbol is to intensify Reiki energy in either side, once each. By doing this, Reiki goes into the head. Locate the spine.

2. Place your index finger and middle finger on either side of the receiver's spine. Quickly slide your fingers down along the spine (from the bottom of the neck to the sacrum). Repeat this about twenty times.

3. Find the indentations on the sacrum. As you did in the neck area, place your thumb and index finger there and again draw the symbol on either side, once each. This sends Reiki through both the upper and the lower body of the receiver. Divide the upper part of the body into five or six areas. First, place your palms on the upper area on either side of the spine, then slide your hands down to the sides of the body. Do the same on the remaining parts.

4. Repeat this three or four times.

5. Rub across the small of the back, sliding your hand from side to side (back and forth) with slight pressure. Repeat about ten times.

6. Outsides of the legs: Start from hip area and brush your hand down along the outside of the leg as far as the ankle. Repeat this three or four times. Do the same on the other leg.

7. Backs of the legs: Start from the back of the thigh. Again, brush your hand down from the bottom of the buttocks to the ankle. Repeat this three or four times. Do the same on the other leg.

8. Insides of the legs: Separate the legs a little. Start from inside the thigh and brush your hand down as far as the ankle. Repeat this three or four times.

9. Do the same on the other leg.

10. Pushing down on the base of the thigh with your left hand, clasp the ankle with your right hand. Using your body weight stretch the back of the knee. Repeat the same on the other leg.

11. Pat all over the back from the shoulders down the rib cage to the lower back and to the buttocks. Repeat this three or four times.

12. Pat down the legs in the same order as in 6, 7, and 8. Start from the outside of the leg, then the back and finally the inside of the leg. Right leg and left leg alternately.

It might sound a little difficult but after you practice this a few times you will find it easy. In the *Jikiden Reiki* seminar this massage is introduced on the second day. We always receive very good feedback from participants especially alternative medical professionals in massage therapies, *Seitai-shi*[18] chiropractors, *Shiatsu* masseurs and aroma therapists. They immediately recognize the effectiveness of this massage in combination with their own practice.

This works also for a person without any massage experience. Because Reiki is radiating from your palms you don't need to worry about your massage skills so much. It works anyway. However, if your massage is done well it will be even more beneficial for the receiver, so it is of course better to practice.

The great feedback we get from these therapists every time confirms for me the authenticity of Reiki treatment and I stand in awe once again at the great legacy of Usui Sensei and Hayashi Sensei.

REMARKABLE RESULTS OF REIKI

As Reiki spread beyond Japan only its 'relaxation' aspect has been emphasized. This may have happened for legal reasons but in a way I think it is a quite natural development and there is nothing wrong in it. Reiki has enormous possibilities and brings us supreme comfort both physically and psychologically.

As I mentioned earlier, Reiki was initially created mainly to treat physical illnesses. In Japan today you cannot claim that

Reiki is a medical treatment unless you are a qualified doctor or certified acupuncturist.[19] Still, we can't deny the effectiveness of Reiki. My mother Chiyoko Yamaguchi practiced Reiki over 65 years and she proved that.

Chiyoko:

"Reiki works really well with burns. I have witnessed a lot of burns cured without leaving scars when treated with Reiki. I remember clearly a boy living in my neighborhood. This three year old had burned his hand while he was alone at home. Playing by the fire he had accidentally burnt himself and the resulting injury was really nasty. Three days had already passed when he was brought to us. The burn had started to fester and his hand had turned bright yellow. Doctors in those days would have simply disinfected the wound and wrapped the hand with bandages. If the boy had been given this conventional treatment his fingers would have become stuck together and dysfunctional. His parents were not fully convinced about Reiki in the beginning but they were desperate.

Anyway I started to work on him with my sister and aunt. To our surprise he fell asleep within 20 or 30 minutes even though his mother had said that he had not slept at all because of the pain. It reassured the parents and they decided to allow the treatment to continue.

We gave the boy Reiki for more than an hour everyday and by the third day the weeping of the wound had eased. Several days later the surface of burnt skin peeled off and fresh skin and fingernails were beginning to regenerate underneath. It was truly motivating for us. I deeply appreciated having the opportunity to deal with such a case. His fingers began to function properly and his parents were really delighted."

Around the same time there was another boy in her neighborhood who suffered burns which were less serious but which received conventional medical treatment from a doctor. His fingers became stuck to the palm of his hand and he ended up having an operation to amputate his fingertips. When you consider medical science in those days, Reiki was unquestionably more effective than the conventional medicine available.

Hayashi Sensei used to say that with Reiki problems are cured from deep inside, and my mother was convinced of this once she had dealt with such burns. This one healed not only on the surface but also from deep inside with the flesh regenerating. My mother Chiyoko had numerous experiences treating such cases.

Chiyoko:
"One of my sons got a burn when he spilled rice porridge on his thigh. I gave Reiki only to the main burnt area and it healed, however I overlooked other smaller burns and these spots still have scars."

I also remember my mother giving Reiki to a young girl in my neighborhood who had been scalded by boiling water leaving terrible burns all over her shoulder. She healed without any scars.

Chiyoko has many stories similar to these. She could talk endlessly about her experiences.

OTHER EXAMPLES OF THE MIRACULOUS EFFICACY OF REIKI

The effectiveness of Reiki treatments is not confined to burns. My mother witnessed countless great results. I would like to recall here some of the cases she found impressive.

A SCRATCH ON THE EYEBALL
Chiyoko:
"My sister-in-law got coal dust in her right eye while traveling on a train. The eyeball was scratched and became inflamed.

Her doctor told her that her right eye was festering and that it would soon affect her other eye. He recommended that she should have the right eyeball removed.

Her mother was totally against the operation and hurried to Kyoto from Ishikawa to convince the doctor to wait and find another way. When she arrived the doctor impatiently told her that the festering was getting worse and worse and he could wait only a couple of hours.

My husband and I gave the girl Reiki continuously for the next couple of hours. When the doctor came back to announce that it was the time for the operation thanks to our Reiki her condition had stabilized so he gave us another two hours to see how she would go. We kept on giving her Reiki and little by little the festering wound got better. She did not have to have her eyeball removed."

A HOLE IN THE THROAT

Chiyoko:

"We had a person from Toyama prefecture who had a hole in his throat. During a previous medical treatment an incision had been made for a tube and it had not healed over. Of course he expected the hole to close after the treatment but a year later it was still open. For hygienic reasons he could not even go to a public bath-house.[20]

We gave him Reiki for a month and to his surprise the hole closed. He was really pleased. He asked a surgeon how difficult it would be to close such a hole and the surgeon said it would be quite unlikely for the skin in the throat area to regenerate because the skin there is very thin. This made him even more impressed with the effectiveness of Reiki.

I realized that this is what Hayashi Sensei had meant when he said, "Reiki cures problems from the bottom up".

My family had patients almost every day. My elder sister's Reiki was highly prized and people often came by car to take her to their home."

AN INJURY

Chiyoko:

"One of the boys in my uncle's family injured his head badly. It was pierced by a nail sticking out on a swing and the injury looked like a pomegranate. His doctor had told the family that he could not guarantee that the boy would survive the night, and yet he was healed by Reiki.

In another case a person swimming in the river suffered a deep cut in the palm of his hand (between his thumb and index finger) from a broken glass bottle. This was also healed completely without any stitches after the Reiki treatments."

ACUTE HEPATITIS

Chiyoko:

"When I was a little girl one of my relatives stayed at our house for a while to receive intensive Reiki. She had acute hepatitis and had started to go yellow. Her doctor told her that she needed to have an injection directly into her artery. However he couldn't find the artery and found it difficult to give her injections so she decided to come to us for Reiki treatments. When she went back to the doctor later he told her that she did not need the injections anymore."

PANCREATIC CANCER

This is a recent case concerning a young man in his mid-twenties. Reiki was responsible for his recovery from pancreatic cancer. In desperation his girlfriend had decided to go to Australia to take a famous Reiki course there so she could help him. One of my friends heard about this and told her she didn't need to go to Australia to learn Reiki but could take a course in traditional Japanese Reiki here in Japan. My friend introduced us and we gave both of them *Reiju* (attunement) and gave her boyfriend intensive Reiki treatments four times a week. Two and a half months later his face was a lot ruddier and he felt much better. He went for a check-up and his doctor gave him a clean bill of health. We hear that he is doing fine now.

TERMINAL CANCER

One person came to us who had wanted Reiki treatments for a long time but his family would not allow it. He had cancer, although his doctor had not told him so, and when he finally came to us it was in the terminal stage. Actually it was too late but still he wanted Reiki, it might at least relieve his great pain and medications were not helping him at all.

We gave him Reiki hoping to reduce the pain even a little. It worked well and showed us that Reiki is effective with cancer-generated pain. This person passed away soon afterwards. We cannot render people immortal with Reiki. Once we are born, death is unavoidable. Yet it is worthwhile giving treatment to those who are in the process of dying if it helps reduce pain, even temporarily.[21]

SOME FREQUENTLY ASKED QUESTIONS

CAN REIKI BE USED ON OTHER LIVING BEINGS?

I am often asked this question, "Is Reiki effective on animals?" Folk want to give Reiki to their pets. I understand that pets are treated as one of the family these days.

There is nothing wrong with the intention, however I don't teach this because I never learned how to give Reiki to animals from my mother and she herself did not learn it from Hayashi Sensei. I don't have pets so I have no experience, my answer is, "It should work. I just don't teach it".

My mother once told me that she gave Reiki to her pet gold fish after joining the first seminar. The fish was weak and not swimming. She had not learned how to lay hands on a fish but came up with her own method. She cupped her hands, scooped out some water and put the fish in this water to give it Reiki. When she put it back in the tank and was amazed to see the fish start swimming. This way she found out Reiki would work for animals. Fish at least.

A lot of my students have done it and they say it works. My mother often commented, "Hayashi Sensei did not especially teach it but I think it is fine to do it."

I don't think we should give psychological treatment to our pets. Some people want to treat their own pets, which are not behaving as they want them to. It is often the case that such problems reside with the owner rather than with their pets.

CAN I SEND REIKI TO AN AREA?

Another question I am often asked is 'can we send energy to a devastated area', a place affected by terrible disaster like an earthquake, a tsunami (tidal wave) or a typhoon. I don't teach this because I have not learned how to send energy to a place rather than to people and I don't think Usui Sensei taught sending Reiki to a situation or an area. Usui Sensei called his healing art 'Shin-Shin-Kaizen-Usui-Reiki-Ryoho' or Reiki treatment to improve Body and Mind. He developed his method to deal with human health, but there is nothing wrong with it if you do it with good intention.

DOES REIKI HAVE ANY CONTRA INDICATIONS?

I am also often asked if there are any situations in which we cannot or should not give Reiki.

For example some of my students have told me that they were taught not to give Reiki to a pregnant woman. I don't see why we can't, Reiki is beneficial not only for mothers but also for their unborn babies. My mother always received Reiki (and gave Reiki to herself) when she was pregnant and it helped her and the whole family very much.

Someone also told me that we shouldn't give Reiki to a person undergoing an operation because it disturbs the efficacy of anesthesia. My family members and I have often sent Reiki to someone on the operating table and I never heard of any ill effect. Reiki is really helpful easing pain after an operation.

It never works in a wrong way. I can say this because of my mother's 65 years of experience. In a cleansing process symptoms sometimes appear to worsen and this might worry some people. However the healing crisis is a necessary part of the process before symptoms are cleared. It is important for Reiki givers to understand this themselves and explain it to their recipients.

Chapter 6:

How Jikiden Reiki Is Taught

CORRESPONDENCES BETWEEN JIKIDEN AND DIFFERENT LEVELS OF WESTERN REIKI

Most schools, which teach the Reiki, reintroduced from the West set up four levels (or degrees). You get attuned in Level 1 and learn three symbols in Level 2. In Level 3 you learn a symbol called the 'Master Symbol' and in the final Level 4 you are trained to be a teacher.

The *Jikiden Reiki* curriculum consists of a different set of levels from those of Western Reiki. You begin with the first two courses — *Shoden* (or the first term) and *Okuden* (or the latter term).[22] After certain conditions are met you can proceed to the next level, the *Shihan-kaku* (assistant teacher) training course that is followed by the *Shihan* (teacher) training. These are in accordance with the levels established by the *Hayashi Reiki Kenkyukai* (institute). By the time my mother learned *Shoden* and *Okuden* from Hayashi Sensei in Ishikawa these levels had already been established in this way.

It is difficult to exactly define the correspondence between *Jikiden Reiki* and Western Reiki but if you insist, two-thirds of *Shoden* could be regarded as Western Reiki Level 1, and one-third of *Shoden* and the whole *Okuden* as Level 2. Then *Shihan-kaku* level could be regarded as Level 3, and *Shihan* as Level 4.

In the beginning, in Hayashi Sensei's day, the first two levels were taught intensively as a five-day course. *The Hayashi Reiki Kenkyukai* granted some people teacher qualifications. I hear that there were no specific seminar style training sessions for these levels, but Hayashi Sensei designated and taught qualified people among those who had completed the *Okuden* and practiced sufficiently. Upon receiving these qualifications participants were given permission to teach as *Shihan-kaku* (assistant teacher) and *Shihan* (teacher). A *Shihan-kaku* was permitted to teach the first *Shoden* course and a *Shihan* was allowed to hold both the *Shoden* and the latter *Okuden* courses.

Hayashi Sensei gave some people permission to teach teachers (*Shihan-kaku* and *Shihan*). In my mother's case she was trained as a *Shihan-kaku* and *Shihan* by her uncle Mr. Sugano with Hayashi Sensei's permission before she moved to Manchuria. (See Chapter 2)

In the *Jikiden Reiki* curriculum I conduct a two and a half day seminar in Japan to teach the *Shoden* and *Okuden* levels as a set course. I give a three, four or sometimes five-day course for non-Japanese students because of the need for translation into another language and sometimes two languages. Basically I apply the systems of *Hayashi Reiki Kenkyukai* but I have amended some of the aspects to suit the times.

SHIRUSHI (SYMBOL) AND JUMON (MANTRA)

In the *Shoden* class you will learn the first symbol and in the *Okuden* class you will learn another symbol and a mantra. In the *Shihan-kaku* (assistant teacher) training one more symbol is taught.

Instead of the terms 'symbol' and 'mantra', we use the original Japanese terms Shirushi, meaning a symbol, and Jumon which can be translated as mantra but I am not sure if they are exactly the same. In the seminar I use the original terms but here

I am using the English words. The difference between Shirushi and Jumon is easy to understand. In Reiki, *Shirushi* is simply to be drawn. *Jumon* on the other hand is for both drawing *and* simultaneously saying a set of words out loud.

The way we teach the symbols might be confusing for those who have already taken Western Reiki, but we are not going to change the style because we have found the ideas behind the symbols in Western Reiki to be quite different.

As I mentioned above one difference I found is that in Western Reiki, *Shirushi*, or the symbols, are said out loud. However what they chant out loud is the *names* of those symbols. I found this a little mixed up. The name is just a name. Some years ago when my friend Arjava took the seminar with my mother he asked her why we didn't say anything when we taught a symbol. I remember this conversation vividly with fond memory of my mother. It was during a break late in the afternoon while we were having a cup of dandelion coffee. My mother broke into a mischievous smile when he asked this question. Picking up a spoon from the saucer she asked,

"You use a spoon to stir your coffee. When you use a spoon, you don't say 'spoon, spoon, spoon....', do you? Spoon is just a name. You don't need to call out its name to stir your coffee. It is the same thing with the symbols."

It is sometimes difficult to see this distinction even for Japanese, so I think it is quite natural for non-Japanese people to mix these two things up. Symbols and mantras have significant meanings and in the seminar I teach the meanings because I find it very important that they be understood.

Let me discuss another difference I found in Western Reiki. I have heard people speak of "being attuned to the symbols". First I could not understand what they meant because for us symbols are not something to be attuned to. We attune people to Reiki, not to symbols. We simply 'introduce' symbols and their significance to the students. Then we tell the students when and how to use them. I do believe that symbols today are often regarded as the most important thing in the practice of Western Reiki. People rely too much on symbols, which are simply just peripheral tools. Reiki itself is much more important than the tools.

The manner in which Usui Sensei acquired these symbols has also been misunderstood. A lot of Western Reiki books have implied that the symbols flashed before Usui Sensei while he was meditating, which makes him seem very mysterious.

Usui Sensei was a spiritually developed person but he was also very down to earth. He did not happen to acquire the symbols this way but rather he studied extensively and took ideas from *Shinto* and from Buddhism to develop those symbols. For example, the symbol used to intensify energy for dealing with *Byosen* was clearly taken from *Shinto.* Another symbol used for dealing with psychological issues was developed from a Sanskrit letter. Sanskrit is an ancient Indian language brought to Japan more than 1000 years ago. As for the Sanskrit letters there has been some discussion as to whether Usui Sensei went to India to study, but I doubt that he did.

In those days it was incredibly difficult for Japanese people to travel to India. Moreover, we have cherished the great ancient Indian philosophies 1000 years or more so I don't think he had to go to India to study them. In the seminar, along with teaching the meaning of each symbol, I teach where each concept contained in the symbols comes from. Many past participants have told me that they find it fascinating.

WHAT HAPPENS IN A JIKIDEN REIKI SEMINAR?

Let me give you a rough picture of what happens in a *Jikiden Reiki* seminar.

As I mentioned before, in Japan the seminar runs for three days. The first two and a half days are for *Shoden*, which is divided into three parts, and the 3rd day is for *Okuden*, which is divided into two parts.

Day 1: ***Shoden* (the first term) Part 1**
The background of *Jikiden Reiki* and the first *Reiju* (attunement)

We teach Part 1 of *Shoden* on the first day.

The day begins with an explanation of the purpose of holding the seminar. After that we talk about the history of Reiki, how Usui Sensei founded it and passed it down to Hayashi Sensei, then how my mother, Chiyoko Yamaguchi, was attuned. During this time we display some precious documents like the photographs taken with Hayashi Sensei and a certificate granted by the *Hayashi Reiki Kenkyukai* (institute).

Then we conduct *Reiju* (attunement) after explaining the way in which it should be received. During the three-day seminar participants receive five *Reijus* from *Shihans* (teachers) and *Shihan-kakus* (assistant teachers). So the more teachers there are present the more *Reijus* the participants receive. Basically in all the procedures we use the style of the *Hayashi Reiki Kenkyukai* except that participants now sit on a chair. When Hayashi Sensei was teaching participants sat on the floor in seiza[23].

The participants are told to sit straight, not putting too much pressure around the *Shimo-Tanden* area (a body energy center located a little below the navel). They are also told to breathe deeply with their eyes closed.

After the room is darkened they recite the *Gokai* (the five principles) in front of a replica of the *Gokai* scroll drawn by Hayashi Sensei. Hayashi Sensei used to tell teachers to conduct *Reiju* in front of the scroll because it has great energy which cleanses the venue. Even today I often hear participants in my seminar say that they feel the energy radiating from the scroll.

I am afraid that I cannot explain how the *Reiju* is conducted here but let me just say it is really powerful. Most participants can feel Reiki penetrating even if it is quite subtle in the beginning.

During *Reiju,* a lot of interesting things happen. Some people see bright light (it is often purple light) and others say that they see some image of Buddha. Interestingly participants from Europe see the Virgin Mary or angels. Maybe each person's image of divinity is a reflection of their religious upbringing.

Some participants claim that they receive *Reiju* from three people when there were only two doing it. The ritual is practiced in a darkened room so they can't see anything, but they definitely perceive the extra person's hands laid upon them. I wonder if Usui Sensei or Hayashi Sensei is helping us and making sure we give *Reiju* correctly.

I don't want the seminars to be taken in order to pursue spiritual experiences, so I am not going to elaborate further. When I hear this kind of feedback I am however sometimes again blown away at how amazing Reiki is. A sense of awe for the great Senseis and their devotion in leaving us this wonderful gift fills me.

After the first *Reiju* is complete we practice *Reiki Mawashi* (Reiki circulating practice). Everyone in the seminar including all the teachers sit in a circle laying their hands on the back of the person in front. We do this for ten to twenty minutes. We have the participants try to feel sensations in their palms to help develop sensitivity in their hands. When we practice this most people in the circle give interesting feedback like "I feel really warm", "Feels so comfortable", "There's a tingling sensation in my hands", or "My hands are burning!" What they are feeling is a variety of sensations of *Byosen,* which I have elaborated upon in Chapters 3 and 5. As mentioned there, when your palms cover troubled areas you get sensations and these sensations change accordingly. Reiki also has the ability to flow into areas that need energy. For example, even though you are laying your hands on someone's shoulders Reiki automatically runs to, say, the kidneys, which for the receiver is a troubled area. Some people experience this even in a short session. We often hear them say, "My problem spot started to ache when you put your hands on my shoulders and then it quickly eased." So this *Reiki Mawashi* practice itself is very effective. It is also a way in which you can simultaneously give and receive treatments.

After the *Reiki Mawashi* participants get a chance to practice Reiki using a treatment table. For those who have learned West-

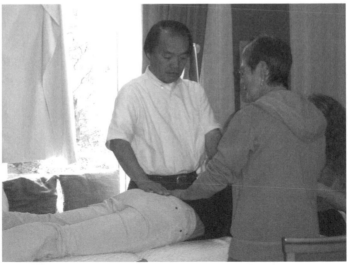

During a Reiki treatment

ern Reiki there may be a surprise when we give instructions. Most Western Reiki schools teach a basic twelve or more specific hand positions for treatments regardless of whether the spot is troubled or not, while, in *Jikiden Reiki* seminars, we guide students to place their hands according to the sensations in their palm. Thus there isn't any specific order in the hand positions. We do however consider the head the most important place to treat and it should never be skipped. When there are more than two practitioners, one remains with his hands on the head of the receiver and the other works on the affected area.

In the seminar we usually have participants give a group treatment to one receiver, so everyone takes charge of one area such as the head, the affected area, the soles of the feet or the back of the knees. When the receiver is lying face down we recommend laying the hands between the shoulder blades, around the kidneys, on the shoulders, the neck and the back of the head. Most people have *Byosen* there. After receiving *Reiju* various sensations in their palms enable participants to detect the *Byosen* in the recipient.

Some people find it hard to sense it right away on the first day, but most can feel it more or less by the end of the seminar. Their perception anyway gets clearer through practicing Reiki every day so they don't have to worry about their sensitivity at that stage. On the other hand there are those who are so sensitive that they actually start feeling pain flowing through their hands from the very first day. They sometimes worry about picking up negative energy from the person they are treating. This does not happen. They are not absorbing negativity but simply sensing *Byosen*, hence when they take their hands away the sensation disappears. Reiki can deal with any level of *Byosen*. Even in the three-day course participants are able to observe the effectiveness of Reiki.

Day 2: *Shoden* (the first term) Part 2 and 3
Introduction of the first *Shirushi* (symbol) and *Kekko* Massage

On the second day we teach two sections—Shoden part two in the morning and part three in the afternoon. The morning class starts with *Reiju* followed by *Reiki Mawashi* (mentioned in Day 1). Following these we introduce the first symbol, which signifies the highest place, that which humans cannot reach which is the source of Reiki. Usui Sensei took it from a *Shinto* concept and it is used to focus energy to tackle *Byosen*. I can feel Reiki energy focused in the area when I use this symbol.

Just as Hayashi Sensei used to do in his seminar, I always advise the participants not to over use this symbol because it is for focusing energy, it makes no sense to use it too often anyway.

After introducing the first symbol we teach another important element of Reiki, the *Ketsueki-Kokan Ho* (or *Kekko*) massage. The words *Ketsueki-Kokan Ho* can be literally translated as 'blood exchange method', but of course it doesn't mean we actually exchange a person's blood. It means that after receiving the massage your blood circulation has improved so you feel as rejuvenated as if all your blood had been exchanged. Please refer to Chapters 3 and 5 for details.

In the afternoon we do another *Reiju* and also *Reiki Mawashi* plus an additional practice method called *Reiki Okuri* (sending Reiki). For this everyone sits in a circle facing toward the center, hands as if joined but not directly touching those of the person sitting on either side. Even though their hands are not touching the participants can feel Reiki flowing from palm to palm. Some describe the feeling as a breeze and others say they feel a magnetic sensation. At this point they have already received three *Reijus* and their Reiki channel is much broader now so the perception of their hands is much keener.

Then it is time to introduce a method for both maintaining and improving the sensitivity required to detect *Byosen* more accurately with ones hands. This method is called *Hatsurei-ho* or the method for radiating Reiki. It is a very simple five-day individual regime that takes 30 to 40 minutes. This enables anyone and everyone to practice Reiki and develop the sensitivity of their palms even when alone. By following this one can become a capable practitioner.

Then we have the participants practice Reiki treatments again using Reiki tables. Most of them are more confident than on the previous day.

Reiki Okuri

Day 3: *Okuden* **(the latter term) Part 1 and 2**
        Seiheki **(psychological) treatment and** *Enkaku* **(distant) treatment**

On the third day we go into *Okuden* (the latter term), which is divided into Part 1 and 2. The day starts with *Reiju* and *Reiki Mawashi*. In the morning we concentrate on psychological issues.

Originally Reiki was designed for physical problems and this is still its main focus. In the old days people had psychological issues of course but they seem to have been minor compared with those of today. Thus even though students learned psychological healing they did not use it as much as we do today. My mother was quite surprised to find that these kinds of issues are so serious now. We have had plenty of feedback on psychological treatment showing just how effective it is. Giving it is very simple and I demonstrate and have everyone experience it in our classes. So it is appropriate introduce the symbol for psychological issues or hidden trauma, which may reside deep in the unconsciousness.

This treatment is very effective for all kinds of psychological problems, like stress issues or eating disorders — anorexia and bulimia. It can also be applied in cases of domestic or alcohol induced violence as well as to a recent and serious social phenomenon here in Japan known as *Hikikomori* (isolationism in young people who avoid social contact and seclude themselves). It also works wonderfully with minor issues like child bedwetting. It would therefore be particularly beneficial for psychologists to learn Reiki. One of my students who is a professional counselor tells me he uses it and it has been very effective.

This treatment is clearly mentioned in *Reiki Ryoho no Shiori* (Reiki Treatment Guidance) published by the *Usui Reiki Ryoho Gakkai*.

Q: Does the Usui *Reiki Ryoho* only heal illnesses?
A: No, as well as being very effective in treating physical illness it is useful for physical weakness or psychological problems including trauma. It is also effective for less severe difficulties such as timidity, indecisiveness, nervousness etc. Once you have resolved these challenges in yourself you gain access to the spirit of Buddha or the divine when healing others, bringing happiness to both you and to those you heal.

In the *Seiheki* psychological healing treatment Reiki works on the receiver's subconscious. To give this treatment the giver draws *Seiheki no Shirushi* (the *Seiheki* symbol over the crown, directing the Reiki energy to the core of the brain. After drawing the symbol the giver says a certain set of phrases out loud or mentally to reverse the negative habit of the receiver. The phrase might sound harsh because it uses 'must' and 'mustn't', taboo wordings in ordinary psychological counseling sessions. However I believe we should use the original phrase, harsh as it may sound even when translated into another language, because it works wonderfully when used with Reiki energy. In this technique we don't work with an affirmation in the western sense of the word, but with a direct command to the receiver's conscious and unconscious mind. In Seiheki treatments givers perceive sensations in their palms. It feels quite similar to the *Byosen,* which is sensed, in physical treatments, however in this situation what the giver perceives is not an accumulation of toxins but the flow of energy. The treatment should continue until these sensations ease or stop. During treatments the receiver also experiences specific sensations. Some people feel a throbbing in the head and others a strong energy flowing in at the head and then tingling in a particular part of their body; still others see a bright light even with their eyes shut.

Treating our own children with this psychological method we need to be aware not to do so with the egoistic motive of molding them into the way we would like them to be.

Extra Information — Jikiden Original Method

SEIHEKI (PSYCHOLOGICAL) TREATMENT USED TO REPAIR BONES, ORGANS AND MUSCLES

While the *Seiheki* treatment is designed to deal with psychological problems, we have also found it effective for resolving bone, muscle and even visceral problems by requesting these to return to their original healthy state using the Reiki energy. This implies that all cells must have consciousness.

Please note my mother Chiyoko did not learn this from Hayashi Sensei, it is our own discovery through our own experience.

In the afternoon we teach *Enkaku* (distance) treatment. This is used for giving Reiki energy to someone at a distance. We introduce a *Jumon* (a mantra-like phrase) for this treatment method while we explain the procedure. As I mentioned previously, the difference between the symbols in Japanese, *Shirushi* and *Jumon*, is very easy to explain. Both are drawn and the only difference is that Jumon has to be drawn and also *said aloud* at the same time. A *jumon*, or mantra, develops its power by being spoken out loud.

An important aspect of the *Enkaku* treatment is how well a sender of Reiki can visualize the receiver. It is best to have a photo of the receiver when sending Reiki to someone you have never met before. If this is impossible get as much information about the receiver as possible. In order to be specific about the person you need to know at least the receiver's full name, their date of birth or age, gender and the symptoms. When all the information is ready project the image of the receiver onto a part of your own body. At the same time draw and say aloud the *Enkaku Jumon*. Then lay your hand on the target area of the receiver projected onto your own body. By doing this the remote Reiki switch is on and the receiver in the distant place will be blessed with Reiki.

In our seminar participants have the opportunity to experience an *Enkaku* treatment. We set up an actual *Enkaku* environment using a divider in the center of the room to separate senders from receivers. They are actually not that far away from each other but they can at least experience giving a treatment to someone they are not directly touching. In practice, when they are being the senders most students get very excited because they feel the *Byosen* even though they are not giving the treatment directly. As receivers many of them feel something going on in their body. Some mention having quite detailed bodily sensations in which they feel strongly pushed or pulled by something invisible.

When my mother learned Reiki 65 years ago not many people had acquaintances in far away places so they did not practice distant healing very often. The exception of course was during World War II. Men were sent to war and the women at home sent Reiki to their husbands, brothers, fathers and sons in the battlefield. They sent energy to heal their loved ones and also used it to confirm whether they were alive or not. As long as they felt *Byosen* they were comforted because it meant that the receiver was alive and receiving Reiki.

Enkaku can be applied in a variety of ways. It is convenient for sending energy to yourself when you want to treat parts of your own body that you can't easily reach, such as your back. It can also be combined with the *Seiheki* psychological treatment. It is particularly useful when dealing with difficult cases where a receiver won't accept his own problem and rejects help. It is also very useful when you want to give a *Seiheki* treatment to yourself.

After the demonstration of *Enkaku* we conduct the final *Reiju* followed by *Reiki Mawashi* and the practice treatment on the Reiki tables.

REIKI KOKAN (REIKI EXCHANGE)

A candle ceremony introduced by Hayashi Sensei

When we have extra time in a seminar we introduce a very short and simple ritual called *Reiki Kokan* or Reiki Exchange. Here the participants are able to feel the great Reiki energy via a ceremony using a pair of candles placed on a low table.

This ritual was introduced by Hayashi Sensei when he came to Ishikawa to hold seminars. The participants are allowed to feel the great Reiki energy. Because he stayed there overnight he had extra time to share with local students in the evenings. I heard that this was originated by Hayashi Sensei not by Usui Sensei. The method helped people with Hatsurei-ho (Reiki radiating) using the candles' fire-energy.

Hayashi Sensei would ask the students to prepare the ceremony, but the things he wanted were nothing special, just a few items that people in those days would have in their homes. In the ceremony a *Shihan* or *Shihan-kaku* sits in a darkened room in front of the scroll, hands joined. Opposite him, across a table with lit candles sits the student.

These candles, one red, one white represent fire and water. Fire symbolizes a vertical energy burning upward and water a horizontal energy, which spreads. These vertical and horizontal energies meet and generate enormous power. A traditional *Shinto* concept helps explain this. Participants usually enjoy this ceremonial atmosphere very much. It really is something quite special.

I used to practice this with my mother when we held workshops but I dropped it after she passed away. Now I have started doing it again in the non-Japanese classes.

To conclude the seminar we give each participant a certificate to show they have successfully completed the course. This traditional Japanese style *Jikiden Reiki* certificate replicates the one issued by the *Hayashi Reiki Kenkyukai*. We inscribe the participant's name with India ink and a brush, which makes it look very impressive.

Completing the course is however just the first step. Living with the *Gokai* (five principles) and practicing Reiki constantly is the key to becoming a good practitioner.

This is why we set up conditions for those who hope to proceed to the next level. After these conditions are fulfilled they can join our *Shihan-kaku* (assistant teacher) and *Shihan* (teacher) trainings to become qualified teachers.

Reiki Kokan.

SHIHAN-KAKU (ASSISTANT TEACHER) AND SHIHAN (TEACHER) COURSES

When Hayashi Sensei taught Reiki the *Shihan-kaku* and *Shihan* levels were not taught in a formal seminar with a set curriculum as we do today. It was then based more on trust. Take my mother's case for example: she learned to give *Reiju* (or attunement) from her uncle Mr. Sugano with the permission of Hayashi Sensei, becoming a *Shihan-kaku,* and later a *Shihan.* However today I give the seminar with a set curriculum for these levels because it is more organized and interactive. I set a few assignments for those who hope to join these courses. For instance, to join the *Shihan-kaku* (or assistant teacher) course I ask you to wait at least six months after you finish the *Okuden* level to give you sufficient time to practice Reiki extensively. You have to give at least 120 hours of treatments to more than 40 different people by the time you join the course because I want you to develop the sensitivity for *Byosen* in your hands before you proceed to the next level. You also have to repeat the *Shoden* and *Okuden* classes at least once to review what you learned before.

In the *Shihan-kaku* seminar today students can learn *Reiju,* which is the main thing in the seminar, and this was what my mother learned from her uncle. For the *Shihan-kaku* level one symbol is introduced. I explain the meaning of the symbol and how we use it. Students have the opportunity to practice *Reiju* with the other participants and I spend a little time on how to conduct seminars because after becoming *Shihan-kaku* they are allowed to start teaching. If they wish to become a Shihan (or teacher), I ask them to gain some teaching experience. I have them teach *Shoden* (the first term) level and then get their students to write feedback on the class. At this level they don't learn any new symbols or mantras.

The *Shihan* course is not given to teach something new. It is conducted so as to review what they are going to teach. In other words the seminar is undertaken to gain recognition as a fully certified teacher. Those who join the seminar will be given a review paper beforehand to see how well they have understood. For this they have to repeat the main courses, *Shoden* and *Okuden,* one more time before joining the *Shihan* course. I think this is important because they will be responsible for teaching people.

In *Jikiden Reiki* I ask people to practice extensively and to complete these assignments before proceeding to the next levels. It might sound a little tough but I believe it is not too hard for those who are serious about Reiki. I believe the most important thing in Reiki is practicing it, so most of the assignments I set are designed to encourage students to practice. I do hope there are going to be a lot of people who can teach *Jikiden Reiki* in the future, both at home and abroad, to make it accessible to as many people as possible. In the future I am going to leave seminars outside of Japan to the teachers there.

REIKI – TRUMP CARD FOR THE NEW MILLENNIUM

Our goals

In *Jikiden Reiki* seminars I always begin by outlining our motives.

These are:

1. To publish illustrations of the effectiveness and document peoples' experiences of Reiki.

2. To enable people to use Reiki as an effective complement to conventional medical care.

156

3. To introduce the effectiveness of Reiki to doctors, nurses and other medical professionals, thereby initiating its use in conjunction with Western medicine in the conventional medical field.

4. To introduce the use of Reiki for medical care in the household. This should help to break dependence on everyday allopathic remedies and conventional drugs. The ultimate objective here is twofold. Firstly people will become healthier as their bodies start to remember how to heal themselves without chemical substances introduced from the outside. Secondly there will be a significant reduction in the amount of medical waste, a positive effect on the environment, which can be global in scale.

When you read Chapter 7 you will find that some *Jikiden Reiki* students, including professional therapists, have already experienced the wonderful effectiveness of Reiki when complimenting conventional medicine. So now we simply have to collect more case studies to convince more medical professionals of its effectiveness.

The first three motives of *Jikiden Reiki* are about the use of Reiki for improving health.

The fourth is about using Reiki on a much broader scale than the three earlier items. It is about Reiki tackling global environmental issues. You might wonder, "How can Reiki improve the global environment?" Once I was asked this question by a colleague I worked with in an environmental organization. This is how I explained it:

"Medical waste generated in the treatment of infectious diseases alone amounts to 120 to 130 tons per 100,000 people per year. In total, annually in Japan, 150,000 tons of such waste is generated. If every household had at least one Reiki practitioner curing half of the illnesses at home the amount of medical waste would be greatly reduced — by roughly 75,000 tons."

Alongside other alternative medicines Reiki has a great advantage: it does not need any tools. It is the ideal alternative for dealing with sicknesses today. All you need is your hands and it doesn't create any waste to pollute the environment.

My efforts to explain the effectiveness of Reiki have been received very well. I was invited to make a presentation to an organization called the Holistic Medicine Forum. This is a network of doctors who are into alternative medicines. I talked to the doctors on Reiki — and its potential use in future medical fields. I hope I was able to make an impression on their outlook.

I also believe that by using Reiki daily we will change the way we view life in general, becoming more attuned to the Universal Energy. The resulting change in our attitudes will cause us to become more environmentally friendly thus helping to mitigate the pressure our modern lifestyle applies on the global environment. The change may be slow but it will be sure.

I am going to continue doing everything I can to pass on this gift from existence, Reiki, to more and more people as the great alternative to today's modern medicine. It will help us make the world a better place — a world without illness and environmental destruction.

I am hoping that this tiny stream of activity will grow into a huge flowing river.

Chapter 7:
Feedback from Jikiden Reiki Students

Case 1
REIKI FOR YOUNG MOTHERS

**Aroma therapists and Jikiden Reiki Kenkyukai Shihans
Kumiko and Saeko Ito (Kyoto, Japan)**

We run a salon for aroma therapy and Reiki treatment in Kyoto. Before learning *Jikiden Reiki* we mainly practiced Qigong healing. One day we had a problem. We picked up 'Jaki' or negative energy from a client while we were practicing Qigong and we began to wonder how we could avoid being affected by negative energy.

Then we met Mr. Tadao Yamaguchi through an environmental group we belonged to. Mr. Yamaguchi belonged to another such group and one day he said he was planning to set up a seminar called *Jikiden Reiki*. We thought it would be helpful to take this seminar so we signed up for it right away.

The very day we received the *Reiju* or attunements we checked each other's energy and were very excited to find that its volume was greatly enhanced.

In our Qigong practice we always felt tired after treating sick clients with our healing methods. Perhaps it was because we were too eager to cure them. Now, with Reiki, we understand that we are just an instrument facilitating the flow of universal energy through our client's body, trusting in the natural healing process. We just try our best and leave the outcome to the universe, so now we don't have to be so anxious. Adopting this selfless attitude is important and we have found that the more selfless we become, the more blessed we are with energy.

Our most notable experience once we started using Reiki is the case of an elderly lady who fell unconscious and was in a critical condition. She was 93 years old and her doctor had told her family that she would not survive the night. In desperation that night at 11pm her daughter called us for help and we hurried to their house to give her a Reiki treatment. At the house the atmosphere was quite intense. Relatives and nurses had already gathered and just then the lady stopped breathing. One of her daughters started reading the Bible to her mother.

We gave her Reiki for about an hour. After laying our hands on her head, feet and stomach area we could feel Reiki flowing. A little while later to our surprise she came around and said quite clearly, "I want to go to the bathroom!"

We hear that she is still alive. Actually this was not a first for her as Reiki had saved her life once before. Her doctor thought she was going die that time also but she survived thanks to Reiki treatment. The doctor was really amazed at how she keeps reviving. He joked with her that she might be immortal. That was when we understood that Reiki can also help older people live out their destined time in good health.

Today a lot of people are seeking healing and aromatherapy is one of the most popular healing methods. When a client comes to our clinic for an aromatherapy treatment because of psychological difficulties we often find potential physical ailments in the spine, liver or kidneys. It is usually the case that these people had not noticed the hidden physical problems. We often hear them say, "I have never had stiff shoulders."

The *Jikiden Reiki* seminar showed us that traditional Reiki can be used to treat people with physical problems. It is also very useful as a preventative measure for those who have potential ailments, which have not yet started to show symptoms. We now combine *Jikiden Reiki,* aromatherapy and 'Sotai-ho' (a very effective exercise method using breathing techniques to repair spinal distortion). For those who are not very sensitive and not able to feel the Reiki energy very well, the gentleness of aromatherapy is a fine complement. Then they say, "I am so relaxed that I don't feel my body at all. I feel like I am in the clouds." Probably the Reiki energy causes them to feel this way.

Some are simply impressed because they have never been treated so well before by another person. We believe this is the result of a combination of the warmth of human hands massaging, effective essential oils made from natural herbs plus Reiki energy. It is an ideal combination for anyone wishing to become a 'genuine healer.'

Aromatherapy is a great method to make people feel relaxed and happy but it doesn't mean that everyone is enchanted. Aroma massage is not the best way for some people who are shy about removing their clothes for an oil massage. For those cases Reiki is ideal. You can apply Reiki simply by laying on your hands or you don't even need to touch the client but can send them energy from a distance. So it can be practiced anywhere, anytime, whether you are interested in your spiritual development or not. Anybody can use it. It is just a wonderful divinely bestowed gift.

Today people lead such hectic lives that they lose touch with themselves and many new problems arise. Human relationships have become shallow. Young people tend to be afraid of getting hurt and are avoiding genuine communication with others.

By using Reiki we can help change these trends. Reiki, as a tool of non-verbal communication, allows people to feel warmth and tenderness both through giving and receiving. A reminder of how wonderfully we can take care of each other.

What we would like to do is introduce *Jikiden Reiki* to young mothers to help in bringing up their young children. Today mothers undergo a great deal of anxiety trying to bring up their little children in this chaotic world where they are exposed to too much confusing information. *Jikiden Reiki* would be very helpful and we would like them to appreciate its effectiveness. Understanding this effectiveness through our own experience we are attempting to reassure these people that it's possible to maintain good health without relying on any medication or vaccination. Reiki practice is helpful in another way. It enables us to spend some peaceful moments laying our hands on ourselves or on someone else, developing consciousness through learning to listen to the messages our body and mind are sending us. We become aware of the importance of nature and of cherishing others and by learning to cherish ourselves.

Whenever we attend a Reiki gathering we learn something new. The whole experience makes us realize that we human beings exist beyond the boundary of human knowledge.

Why don't you come and join us?

Kumiko and Saeko Ito

Case 2

SIMPLE YET PRACTICAL!

Before and after learning Jikiden Reiki
**Therapist, Jikiden Reiki Kenkyukai Shihan
Sandy Catford (Canterbury England)**

I work in a clinic in the city of Canterbury with a beautiful view
of the Cathedral from my window. There are a few different
practitioners here doing Acupuncture, Hypnotherapy, Massage
and so on, but the place is primarily known for Herbal Medicine.
The dispensary is really old and traditional. It does you good
just breathing in all the gorgeous herbal aromas when you walk
through the door!

Eventually I'd like to open a Reiki 'shop' on the High Street.
With a couple of practitioners, one for regular bookings and one
to talk to and treat people who just turn up to try it out. It would
certainly give a lot of people access to Reiki. One day!

I first learned Reiki from a master here in the UK. He is
a wonderful teacher with a deep respect for the traditional aspects
of Reiki. Whilst learning I absorbed information like a sponge.
I think I read every Reiki book in print (well in English anyway…), but it was the writing of Frank Arjava Petter that I really
liked. I admired the way that he questioned some of the historical 'facts' surrounding Usui Sensei and the foundation of Reiki.

When I met and got to know Arjava he became my teacher and friend and I traveled to Japan to train with him. His teaching is powerful and opened up another dimension to the energy for me. It was through his introduction that I met Mrs. Yamaguchi and Tadao Yamaguchi and was able to train with them both in Kyoto. I feel very lucky that life took me along that path!

I'm not comfortable with the politics that surround Reiki in the UK. "This way's better", or "that way's better", or in some cases "this is the **only** way". I can't join in with that. So when I say how much I enjoy *Jikiden Reiki* I'm being careful not to compare it with what's available in the West. Yes, it is very different and I prefer it to the system of Reiki I was taught originally. But Western Reiki was and is wonderful too. My treatments before learning Jikiden were extremely effective and I felt the flow of energy really strongly. But now it is different. There is a practical, down-to-earth feeling about what I do. It's simpler and feels like some of the 'packaging' has been removed. Some of the extra ideas that we've added here in the West have always seemed a little strange to me, so it was a relief to leave them behind!

So when I was trained to attune others and eventually to *Shihan* level to be able to teach Jikiden I was happy to find that students who had learnt other forms of Reiki also felt this same 'earthiness' — it wasn't my imagination. (Isn't self-doubt wonderful? Keeps us on our toes!)

But… (sorry, there is a 'but'!)… for a Westerner to come to grips with the real Japanese Reiki does require a certain broadening of attitude. There is no doubt that Western and Japanese people see things from a slightly different viewpoint. Here in the West we're very language-based, whereas a lot of the Reiki thinking is concept-based and can't be described in mere words. ("The best thoughts cannot be said, the second best thoughts can only be misinterpreted"- Bert Hellinger, one of my other favorite people). Feeling Reiki, doing treatments and in particular meditation have really helped me understand my training more. The secret, if there is one, is to allow Reiki to seep into all areas in your life. It's easy to have little pockets of special 'sacred' times in the day, but to let Reiki affect the humdrum and downright nasty bits of the day too — now that's an interesting challenge. Just remembering is a meditation in itself. The next time you're in the queue in Sainsbury's try letting Reiki flow. Mrs. Yamaguchi was probably the most 'normal' person I've ever met. She had no need to make any impression on me, she just 'was'. At the same time she was the most powerful person I'd ever met. I miss her. I'm so happy that Tadao Sensei is taking her teaching to the world. He's the walking embodiment of her spirit and he's so committed to seeing Reiki thrive in a world that needs it so much.

I have really loved my trips to Japan, but apart from being a fascinating and fun place to visit, the whole atmosphere and attitude there helped me absorb the training into my system.

So, from a practical point of view, how have things changed since the Jikiden training?

Well I feel that my hands are easier to read now. There are different sensations, depending on the problem in the body, other than just heat. I scan a lot but often incorporate this into a standard treatment. One regular client commented as soon as I got back from my first level training that the session was stronger.

Personally I feel really lucky that I've found something that makes me so happy. Reiki touches every part of my life. To be able to experience such a pure and traditional 'craft' is a real privilege.

My way of repaying the universe for introducing me to such a gift is to follow the five principles the best I can. In particular Hito ni shinsetsu ni' (be kind to others). I learnt from my training with Chiyoko Sensei that the true meaning of this is to give Reiki to people. What could be a better life's work?!

Sandy Catford

Case 3

MEDICAL INSTITUTIONS IN NEED OF REIKI

Practicing chiropractor,
Jikiden Reiki Kenkyukai Shihan-kaku
Masahiro Nawae (Kyoto, Japan)

I used to be a nurse and now I am a chiropractor. I have been in practice for twelve years.

About two or three years ago I noticed that I always felt exhausted after work at my clinic. I wondered if I could find a suitable way to deal with this fatigue. One day one of my clients suggested that I should learn Reiki. I had never heard the word before so it didn't click with me. My client knew it by name only and had no further information.

So I checked through books and websites until found that Reiki could give good results merely by laying hands on people. This grabbed me because it would not only be good for me but also very useful in my work too. However, I was not so sure that one could obtain such an ability by merely receiving 'Reiju' or attunements. Of course it would be ideal for me if I could master something so amazing without going through some long and difficult training. To be honest part of me did not totally believe in it until I joined the seminar.

I kept checking around for information about Reiki and learned that Usui Sensei, the founder of Reiki, attained enlightenment and found Reiki on Mt Kurama in Kyoto. This made me very excited because I was born in Kyoto and grew up there. I felt like I was led to Reiki by some invisible agent and my mind was set on joining a seminar to learn Reiki.

After some research I chose *Jikiden Reiki* as I found this is where traditional Japanese style Reiki is offered. I was curious and also anxious about what I could learn in a three-day seminar and it turned out to be amazing. I started using Reiki on my clients from the very day following the seminar and I was happily surprised at how effective it is.

One client came with stiff shoulders. I gave Reiki to the muscles of both her shoulders where I could find stiffness and pressure pain. I was able to detect the 'Byosen' or problematic area very clearly. It was much stronger than I had experienced in the practical training in the seminar. A tingling sensation ran through the center of my palms and when I removed my hands the tingling disappeared. When I laid my hands back on the shoulders I felt the tingling sensation again. Then I was confident that I had found the 'Byosen' with my hands.

The client told me that she felt very warm and thought that I had used some electrical equipment. After a while my hands became warm but the tingling sensation in the palms eased.

After holding my hands on her shoulders for about ten minutes I checked the stiffness with my fingers. It was exciting to find that it seemed to have melted and her shoulder muscles were relaxed and flexible. At the end of the treatment the client herself felt much lighter in the shoulders. It was so amazing to be able to use Reiki only one day after I finished the seminar.

Another client had a terrible backache and couldn't bend her body. It was caused by some muscle problems in her buttocks.

She felt pain when I pressed the buttocks so I started giving Reiki around the area. When I laid on my hands I felt a dull pain in the palms, which traveled, up to my wrists. I was confident that it was 'Byosen'. This 'Byosen' was clearly different from that of the previous client with stiff shoulders.

This client also felt warm and comfortable. Fifteen minutes later the heavy pain in my palms disappeared and I started to feel a throbbing sensation as though the muscles in her buttocks were contracting. After a while it stopped and the sensation in my palms changed, becoming weaker and I could feel only a little warmth.

When the sensation eased I asked my client to stand up and bend her body forward and backward. She exclaimed that she felt no pain. Actually I was more surprised than she was.

I was just amazed to witness the effectiveness of Reiki with my own eyes just one day after the seminar. To tell the truth at that point I could not really grasp a sense of Reiki actually flowing through me. Still, I felt the warmth and Byosen in my palms so I accepted this as a fact and kept working on developing sensitivity.

As a chiropractor I practice mainly on those who have problems with their muscles, bones and nervous system. I intend using Reiki actively not only for these aspects of the body but also for internal organs and for psychological problems.

My original purpose in learning Reiki had been to deal with my own fatigue after work. In fact Reiki has been very effective for me also. When I go to bed I give myself Reiki from my head to those other parts of my body that I can reach while lying down. It makes me feel really good. I used to have trouble sleeping but when I do this I fall asleep before I know it. Then in the morning I wake up easily feeling refreshed.

These days I start the day without any tiredness hanging over from the previous day so I can concentrate better than before on my clients. My work has become less stressful.

I believe it is very important for a practitioner like me to maintain good physical condition. Without this it is difficult to help other people recover from their complaints. I am really grateful that I learned Reiki. It is like a win-win situation for me, useful for my chiropractics work and helpful for dealing with my fatigue.

As I mentioned before I used to work as a nurse. From this perspective I really hope that Reiki will be practiced in hospitals. I hear that in some countries in the West this has already happened, which is wonderful. I do hope this trend will cause us to revaluate our traditional healing methods of 'Te-ate', or hands on healing.

Much like Reiki the art of chiropractics is also an effective alternative medicine. As a practitioner who believes in alternative medicine I am motivated to help people using methods that I know work from my own experience. I would like to see Reiki used in medical institutions and in homes, and I am ready to promote *Jikiden Reiki* to the world to see this happen.

Masahiro Nawae

Case 4

REALIZING THE AUTHENTICITY OF JIKIDEN REIKI

Massage therapist Tomoko Griffin
(Auckland, New Zealand)

I am Japanese and I live in New Zealand with my Australian husband.

Around 1998 when I was learning a massage treatment method in New Zealand I happened to hear my classmates talking about Reiki. I asked what it was and I was surprised to learn that it originated in my home country, Japan. When I lived there I knew nothing about it. I went on and learned Reiki and started using it in my massage practice.

One day one of my acquaintances told me that a mutual friend, Claire Morison, wanted to go to Japan to study Reiki, but not speaking Japanese she needed someone to go with her who could help her with the language.

I thought it would be intriguing to learn Reiki directly from a Japanese teacher and anyway it would be nice to visit my homeland for the first time in five years so I offered to go with Claire and help her with the language.

I joined a *Jikiden Reiki* seminar in late 2002. It was really convincing. Thanks to Mr. Yamaguchi's clear explanations all the

170

questions I had had about the many contradictions in the history of Reiki as reported in books written by Westerners were answered.

_ ~ _

I have had a problem with my neck. During *Reiju* my neck ached. I felt the Reiki energy flowing there, which reconfirmed that area's weakness.

In one *Reiki Mawashi* practice (a way of practicing to feel the flow of Reiki by sitting in a circle, placing ones hands on the person in front) I was fortunate to sit in front of Chiyoko Sensei so she laid her hands on my back. When she did this I felt the energy climb up to my neck where the problem was. She moved her hands to the edge of my shoulder blades. Her hands were so warm they made me feel very comfortable. Something deep reached into the core of my body.

The two and a half day course went very quickly but the content of the course was very solid. It was well worth coming all the way from New Zealand.

As soon as I returned to New Zealand I began giving *Jikiden Reiki* treatments to my clients and I clearly felt much stronger energy between my palms even when I made Gassho hands (hands joined as in prayer) at the start of the treatment. After finishing a treatment on a client's back I was rather surprised to see that the area had reddened as if a steam towel had been placed there.

I gave *Jikiden Reiki* treatments to those on whom I had previously practiced Western Reiki and most of them commented that the heat they felt during the sessions had become much more intense and the energy went in much more deeply, more smoothly and with more focus after I came back from Japan.

Before I started practicing *Jikiden Reiki* most of my clients would come to my clinic just for relaxation. Since the seminar in Japan lots of them have told me that their symptoms, various aches and pains have been noticeably relieved.

I also work as a masseuse in a clinic. *Jikiden Reiki* helps me to be more effective with my massage therapy too.

I am still not experienced enough to talk about the effectiveness of *Jikiden Reiki*, but I would like to mention one thing, that the beauty of *Jikiden Reiki* is in its authenticity.

As you might know, Usui Sensei founded Reiki as a treatment method and called it 'Usui Reiki Ryoho' (treatment method). From this we can see that the original aim of Reiki was to treat people with illnesses. In the Western world today Reiki is regarded as some kind of 'spiritual healing method'. The original purpose was rather more simple.

I am so grateful that I had a chance to learn the Reiki passed down directly from Hayashi Sensei. It was supremely meaningful for me to travel all the way back to Japan.

Tomoko Griffin

Case 5

REIKI WITH CHIYOKO SENSEI AND TADAO SENSEI

Jikiden Reiki Shihan
Amanda Jayne (England)

As I made my way up to the 7th floor apartment in Kyoto, the higher the lift went up, the faster my heart beat. This could have been because I always feel uncomfortable in very high buildings but I knew it wasn't. I am really not quite sure why I was so nervous about meeting Chiyoko Yamaguchi and her son Tadao, after all I had learned Reiki before. But there was no denying that, along with the interesting drumming sounds going on in my chest, my stomach was making some very strange noises by the time I arrived at their front door.

As I entered the apartment I saw Chiyoko Sensei sitting in a chair smiling and I felt the warm, inviting atmosphere. My nervousness dissolved completely and I knew that these were the people I wanted to study Reiki with. All I wanted to do was hug this lady who gave off such a bright, loving energy but I managed not to launch myself at her—well for a few hours anyway.

The seminar I attended (in 2002) over the next three days was one of the greatest and most exciting experiences of my life. I felt

173

and learned things that I never had before and it happened in a very simple, relaxed and caring way. I went on to study further with Chiyoko Sensei and Tadao Sensei and continued to be amazed at their wealth of experience and knowledge regarding Reiki treatments.

What impressed me most about Chiyoko Sensei was the fact that she was spiritually aware, often seeing wonderful things during attunements, yet she was a very down to earth, balanced person just like everyone's favorite grandmother... humble, caring and primarily concerned with the wellbeing of her family and those around her.

I remember her saying that Westerners "think too much". At first this seemed a cultural idea that I didn't really agree with. However, through learning and practicing the Reiki she and her son Tadao Sensei taught me, and through reading books and trying out different ways of 'being' for myself I have discovered that I do agree with her. The constant questioning and debating over what and who is right and wrong; the agonizing over what we should do or should have done is not at all helpful to us or to our psychological and physical health. I am not advocating the abolition of questions – of course some questions are important, but maybe looking inside, and paying attention to our instinctual feelings about what is right for us would help us see things in more simple terms.

Sometimes Westerners would come to visit Chiyoko Sensei and I remember how struck she was by people's apparent need to complicate things. My gradual passive understanding of this became more personal when I tried to help translate the wording of a *kotodama* for the psychological healing work. Two of us agonized over the wording as the exact translation sounded harsh and we found that some Westerners would not accept it. I knew it worked very well because I had done it on myself many times, but there were still questions. Ikuko, my Japanese friend explained to me that the wording was also harsh in Japa-

174

nese, and over time I realized that if you try something and it works well, why change it? And why question it? My cultural background has taught me to question everything and I am grateful for that. It has led me to think for myself, but I realize now that the key lies in recognizing when my questions have already been answered. If I try something and it works and it feels good, then there is my answer.

Both before and since Chiyoko Sensei's death, Tadao Sensei has also been my teacher. There have been many times when I asked a hundred questions about things he said, things I have heard about Reiki or I have misunderstood because of the language barrier. But he always answers every question with humility and integrity. I seem to leave each meeting feeling a little more humble myself and hopefully a little wiser. I have come to believe that, like his mother, Tadao Sensei really cares deeply about others. While he teaches primarily from a perspective of practical treatments, the spirituality is all there if you choose to pursue it or want to ask questions about it. It is not separate from ordinary, everyday life but part of it. I see that he wants to help others on their journey whatever it may be, but he also wants to allow them the freedom to find the path for themselves.

To be honest, there have been times recently when I have felt frustrated listening to people discussing, or reading lengthy disputes on the internet about the exact history of Reiki or which type of Reiki is 'right'. I mean no disrespect to the people involved at all. I believe the whole point of life is to choose whatever feels right, given that there are so many ways to do everything. I am profoundly grateful to Usui Sensei and Hayashi Sensei. However for me the finer details of the history are not as important as my learning how to treat myself and others now, and discovering who I am and what I choose to be next.

I have changed profoundly over the last few years, since living and working in Japan. My family and friends mention it every time I go back to England. I feel very different too and my whole outlook on life has changed. I finally feel like I am on the path to being somewhere and someone I want to be. I have realized that the many things that aren't working in the world today can be changed if we just start by changing ourselves. There are many ways to do this and Reiki is one of them. It has helped me start this part of my journey and has proved invaluable. The simplest things are the most powerful. Having healed so many of my feelings about my turbulent past and the ailments and habits it left me with, I now feel free to help others help themselves too. I am so happy that I listened to my feelings when I nervously entered that apartment on the 7th floor three years ago. I am also happy that the present seminar house is only on the second floor!

Amanda Jayne

A NEW FLAME

Jikiden Reiki Shihan
Silke Kleemann (Germany)

My first contact with Jikiden Reiki was through Frank Arjava Petter who had studied this lineage with Chiyoko Sensei and Tadao Sensei. He talked with much respect about his visits in Kyoto and I could feel that his amazing clarity and simplicity in the Reiki work had something to do with this approach to practicing and understanding Reiki. I had already done my master training with Arjava, but when he told me in the summer of 2004 that Tadao Sensei would come to teach at his house in Düsseldorf, I didn't hesitate. I wanted to get in touch myself with this man who had a lifetime's experience of Reiki, who had literally been raised with Reiki.

The atmosphere was full of expectation. Nearly twenty students had come from all over Europe and all of them were experienced Reiki practitioners who were themselves teaching. Tadao Sensei spoke in Japanese while his assistant Ikuko translated into English, whereupon Arjava translated into German. Linguistically also the course was a real adventure. It was amazing to hear how natural Reiki was for Tadao, it was something he had known all his life. In his family allopathic medicine was never used, not even plasters for the kids. Everything was treated with Reiki. On the other hand, he also seemed to be surprised at our surprise. Some of the questions posed by us Westerners who really think a lot, were hard for him to understand.

For the initiations we sat in three lines of chairs, feet on the ground and hands in Gassho position. Each day we received not only one, but four initiations: one after the other from Tadao Sensei, Arjava Sensei, Ikuko and another Japanese student, Hideko, who already had the degree of *shihan-kaku*, an assistant teacher. So during the five-day course there were a total of twenty initiations for each of us. No wonder I felt like I was burning from the inside out! The initiations felt different from the Western ones. Somehow more connected to the earth, a dry, heavy heat. Especially in my heart I felt how a beautiful, powerful flame was lit, a flame that grew a little stronger each day, with each initiation and with the exercises, which we practiced to refine our sensitivity.

One thing became very clear in the seminar: *Jikiden Reiki* is meant to be applied. Each day we finished with group treatments and Tadao Sensei encouraged us to give as many treatments as possible. He and his late mother used to work a lot with ill people and achieved good results. My first course with Tadao motivated me also to work more with people, and during the following year I was able to observe how my Reiki practice began to change. I grew much more confident working on physical problems (while for more abstract situation-related problems I am still very happy to know the great Reiki applications developed in the West). My regular Reiki partners could feel the difference too. The energy is earthier, more grounded. Even for distant Reiki I now nearly always use the slightly different *Jikiden Reiki* technique, which in my experience is more effective, at least on the body level.

All this had me looking forward very much to Tadao Sensei's second visit to Düsseldorf in the summer of 2005. I wanted to repeat the Jikiden 1 and 2 courses and I also wanted to become a *Shihan-kaku*, so I could give this wonderful initiation myself. The first day on the train from Cologne, where I live, to Düsseldorf I suddenly felt the flame in my heart begin to burn again. This went on for the whole day while I was listening once again to Tadao and his family's Reiki story. Over the course of the seminar the burning didn't get as intense as in the first year, but I had the strong feeling that now the Reiki energy was working on finer levels. I had many valuable insights, understanding some of the tricks of my ego. I felt closer to the Japanese way of thinking and could delight in Tadao's further explanations of the *Shinto* and Buddhist backgrounds of Reiki. Most importantly I could feel everything more intimately. It had been well worthwhile practicing the new techniques for a year before taking the next step. Today I am very thankful to be walking this path — and especially to be collaborating on this book. I am looking forward to what comes next!

Silke Kleemann

"ARIGATO" FROM THE TRANSLATOR

Jikiden Reiki Shihan
Ikuko Hirota (Hyogo, Japan)

Ikuko together with Tadao and Arjava

In the spring of 2002 a co-worker at my old job who is also a very good friend, Amanda Jayne from England, asked me if I had ever heard of Reiki. I still recall this scene clearly. We were in the photocopy room in our office. She told me that it was Japanese. Yes, it sounded Japanese, but I had never heard the word before and my first impression of it, 'Reiki', was not very positive. In my mind I was saying, "What kind of freaky cult-like thing is she talking about?" (This is what most Japanese people today would think). Seeing my reaction Amanda decided not to discuss it any further.

However a couple of months later I had a terrible headache at work and she took this opportunity to try out the Reiki she had learned somewhere. Dubious about what she had said about it I just let her try it. (I was anyway too sick to say no). To my surprise, I could feel the relaxation when she laid her hands on my forehead and within a few minutes I fell asleep in the chair. Afterwards the pain in my head had certainly decreased. These ten minutes convinced me, and the same evening I started to search for information about Reiki on the Internet.

It was a surprise to find a big list of Reiki schools on the net. *Jikiden Reiki* website was in the list too. I had no idea which school would suit me, I just used my intuition. The word 'Jikiden', which roughly means 'original teaching' attracted me. (How simple!) I also liked their website which was quite unsophisticated and not at all decorative, but very down-to-earth. I decided to take their course in the following month, in August 2002. Amanda was very excited (more excited and curious than I was) to hear my decision. She was also interested in learning Reiki with the Yamaguchis and wanted to join the next seminar for non-Japanese people to be held in October.

Later we started to help Tadao Yamaguchi Sensei with translation of e-mail messages coming from foreign countries and in his seminars for non-Japanese students. We were even given the opportunity to help with the translation of some parts of Tadao Sensei's first book in which he collaborated with Frank Arjava Petter Sensei — *The Hayashi Reiki Manual* published in 2003. In the beginning, I was a bit overwhelmed by these opportunities, which came to me so suddenly one after another. I had originally taken up Reiki simply to help myself and the people around me. Since then however I have made so many wonderful friends around the world through Reiki. In every seminar where I translate I learn something valuable from people in the class. I get pretty nervous about my translation before a seminar, but when I see the warm smile of the participants I relax. And when I'm struggling to find an appropriate word to express what Tadao Sensei has said they always try to help me. This exchange creates a very warm atmosphere in the room and I can feel that I am not doing this alone. I enjoy these moments. Sometimes I get frustrated trying to explain something Japanese that cannot be described in words and which I find impossible to verbalize explicitly for people from overseas. But one thing I have noticed is that translating word for word in the seminars is not the most important thing because we understand each other with our hearts. Participants understand the most important things anyway without going via words. Perhaps what they find hard to understand is anyway peripheral to the practice of Reiki. Reiki is universal and, as Tadao Sensei puts it, it is not something, which is given at the seminars, it is already there, in us, so really we know it regardless of the language we speak. I am beginning to understand this.

Then I was given the chance to translate this book from Japanese into English. When I heard this it seemed way beyond my capacity. However, I decided to stop thinking too much in my head and to go with the ideas of *Gokai,* my version. I translated a page each day and did my best 'just for today', beginning in January 2005. Still, even though I finished most of it by early summer, I was quite unsure if the book would really materialize. There had been no way for me to know that later on I would be struck by witnessing with my own eyes how the universe works so beautifully. When I went to Düsseldorf, Germany for Tadao Sensei's seminar in late June. Frank Arjava Petter Sensei kindly proposed Ms. Silke Kleemann as editor for our original edition. She was joining the seminar there to become *Shihan-kaku.* Silke is a wonderful editor whom Arjava Sensei trusts with his own books too. She gave us brilliant ideas and suggestions. I was also very happy when I got the final manuscript from Neehar Douglass after he had used his magic, rewriting it into flowing English. There has been such a wonderful collaboration to bring the book into being—Tadao Sensei, Arjava Sensei, Silke, Monika Jünemann from Windpferd Verlag, Neehar and Nirda, my friend Amanda, Tadao Sensei's secretary Hideko, those *Jikiden Reiki* students who agreed to update their reports and all the other good Reiki friends around the world who encouraged me, saying that they are excited about the book (and you dear reader).

In addition to the original Japanese book, which was published in 2003, we wrote a new chapter to introduce some of the Japanese spiritual culture. It was Silke's suggestion that we should write this for non-Japanese readers and it has become the most intriguing part of the work for me. Through working on this section which is aimed at non-Japanese readers I noticed something — we Japanese don't know much about our own culture, and actually it is we who need first to appreciate it. I must confess that I was not an exception. I grew up in a big city in an already modernized Japan. In the generation that witnessed the economic prosperity of the 1980-90's, here, as a young girl, I knew only the materialistic face of my country. In my 20s and early 30s I was more interested in other cultures. Japanese culture I would turn down as shallow. I was totally thrilled when I (re-)encountered the spiritual side of my own culture through learning Reiki. It was like a happy reunion with the traditional values of "respecting the invisible side of life" which was still cherished in my grandparents' time. In the past half century Japan underwent such a dramatic change that people today seem to have forgotten what it used to be like.

Anyway, I came to understand that there are no shallow cultures anywhere in the world. Through communicating with the wonderful people I have met over these past years I have learned more and more that deep inside we are not so different even though we might be quite different on the outside.

The differences are good too, they help us become aware that our way is not the only way. Once we understand this we can see things from different points of view, and it is a great liberation from the fixed ideas we tend to be stuck with. I learned it through Reiki.

Recently I happily became aware of the reason why I had learned English and translation when I was younger. Maybe subconsciously I knew that I would be given this incredible opportunity. The translating was so much fun that time seemed to just disappear when I was doing it. I never tired of it at all even though it has taken up all my free time for the past year.

I would like to express my deepest respect for all the founders of Reiki and the wonderful legacies they have given us. I would also like to express my gratitude to Tadao Yamaguchi Sensei who trusted me and with kindness gave me the opportunity to translate his book. If there are poor renditions of his words in this book it is due to my poor translation not to Tadao Sensei's original writing.

Last but not least I would like to thank YOU for reading this work. Without you it is not complete.

Thank you very much!
Ikuko Hirota
December 2006

Final Words

I hope I have been able to explain my motivation for spreading Reiki and help you toward a further understanding. It becomes more and more clear how fortunate I have been to live with Reiki helping in every aspect of my life. It has been the most natural thing for me and I have no doubts as to its effectiveness. My sincere wish has always been to introduce the wonder of it to as many people as possible, but it has been a struggle to get people to accept something so 'new'.

At first glance Reiki tends to be regarded as something mysterious or religious. This image precedes its true practical value. As I have mentioned so many times in this book, Reiki has supported me throughout my life. I grew up without relying on the medications that people today so heavily depend upon. They see doctors and take medicine if they catch a cold, and use ointments without a question when they hurt themselves.

There is this fixed idea that only medicines can cure their problems. The only way that I can see to change this implanted belief is to have a lot of people experience Reiki for themselves. I and my children grew up with my mother's supportive Reiki, so we know its greatness from our own experience.

For years I had a growing sense of urgency that something needed to be done or it would die out as just a secret art existing only within one family. My mother was already quite elderly and she would be leaving us one day. I wasn't getting any younger either! I didn't know if my children would follow the Reiki path because they are free to choose their own careers. Furthermore I regard it as my mission to introduce people to the Reiki my mother learned directly from Hayashi Sensei — not only as a relaxation technique but as a great complimentary medicine to be used in their daily life.

It was about 35 years ago that I first shared with others the vision of a life without medicine. There were some young people of my own age at a spiritual meeting who were asking senior members for advice on how to explain to their teachers and friends why they don't take any medicine. On a school excursion one of them got sick on the bus and his teacher had tried to give him a motion sickness pill. He couldn't explain why he didn't want it. I was really excited to find someone with similar experience. I was so happy that I can still remember the excitement at finding people to share my vision with.

This inspired me to study many other important issues, including the harmful side effects of medicines, general environmental issues and organic agriculture without chemical fertilizers. It was at this time that I happened upon the book 'Silent Spring', by Rachel Carson. It had a great and life changing impact on me. The foundations of my activities today are built upon these early experiences.

This new millennium is the century for humanity. People are tired of their hectic modern lifestyles and in great need of healing. Reiki is finding acceptance as an important part of this trend.

It may simply be taken as a way to relax, which is fine, but I am going to pursue my goal of having Reiki used in all medical spheres as a great alternative medicine. In all humility I am going to make every effort to contribute to making the world a better place to live in.

Last but not least, I would like to express my thanks to those who have helped me write this book.

In deep gratitude,
Tadao Yamaguchi

About the Author and Contact Information

Tadao Yamaguchi, born in 1952 in Kyoto, Japan is the son of Chiyoko Yamaguchi, who was the disciple of Dr. Chujiro Hayashi. Tadao lives in Japan and teaches Reiki worldwide. Together with Frank Arjava Petter he wrote *The Hayashi Reiki Manual*, published by Lotus Press.

Contact information:
Jikiden Reiki Kenkyukai Office
c/o Shinyu-do
Aburanokoji Nishiiru AyanoKoji-dori
Shimogyo-ku Kyoto, Japan 600-8478
Fax: 0081 (0)75 343 0064

Jikiden Healing Center Tokyo (Seminar Room)
8-3-5 Haramachida Machida
Tokyo, Japan 194-0013

http://www.jikiden-reiki.com
e-mail: office@jikiden-reiki.com
linking UK website: http://www.jikidenreiki.co.uk

There are also teachers of Jikiden Reiki all around the world, so if you need to find a teacher in your location please contact us for information.

Notes

1 Sensei means "respected teacher."
2 There is an explanation of the Japanese writing system at the end of Chapter 4.
3 *Reiki Ryoho no Shiori*' or Reiki Treatment Guidance—an instruction booklet published by *Usui Reiki Ryoho Gakkai*. If you are interested in reading this book please refer to the translation: '*The Original Handbook of Dr.Mikao Usui*', *by Usui/Petter*, Lotus Press.
4 *Shoden:* 1st grade is more or less equivalent to Western Reiki 1st level. *Okuden:* further grade and is more or less equivalent to Western Reiki 2nd level. For more information see chapter 6.
5 In Japan it has been customary for a bride's family, especially wealthy ones, to provide a set of new luxurious furniture.
6 Military leader of the Samurai caste.
7 *Chiba Tsunetane* (1118 to 1201)—-a Samurai warrior who flourished in the 12th century in Chiba (near Tokyo). He is well known to Japanese historians. His descendants often carried a name taking part of his name —"tane." Usui Sensei's father's name was "Tane-ji."
8 *An-Jin-Ryu-Mei*— a state of complete peace of mind—no fear, no anxiety, not disturbed by anything. This concept was originated in Confucianism and later spread as a basic principle of *Zen* Buddhism.
9 Here they were called *Shihans* but these 20 *Shihans* were given permission to teach other *Shihans*. In those days they used the same word for the two different types of teacher. In Japanese this notion is quite ambiguous. It is something that is quite difficult to explain in writing and may be frustrating for Western readers. However, later generations gave this level a new name— 'Dai-Shihan' meaning 'Big teacher' to distinguish it from the usual *Shihans*.
10 This article is published in its entirety in *The Hayashi Reiki Manual* by Frank Arjava Petter and Tadao Yamaguchi, Lotus Press. Please refer to the book for more information.
11 *Waka* is the general term for classical Japanese verse which consists of 5-7-5-7-7 syllables.
13 The Japanese word *Seiheki* means "habit", "inclination" or "natural disposition."
14 If you would like to learn the *Gokai* in Japanese you can hear them spoken on the CD, *Reiki Space of Peace and Love* by Merlin's Magic, Inner Worlds Music.

15   *Tokugawa Shogunate:* started by *Ieyasu Tokugawa* who successfully took over the rule of Hideyoshi Toyotomi who achieved the unification of Japan in mid 16th century. Ieyasu Tokugawa started his administration in Edo (now Tokyo). He assumed the old title of *Shogun* (military leader). Then the long lasting *Tokugawa Shogunate* started (in 1603). The successful policies of the Tokugawas' successive rulers enabled them to stay in power for the next 250 years, until the mid-19th century.

16   The Meiji Restoration was the recovery of the Imperial prerogatives in the late 19th century which brought feudalism and the shogunate system to an end. With it began the modernization and industrialization of Japan.

17   You can find an exact sequence with photos of this technique in *The Hayashi Reiki Manual,* page 53 ff.

18   Therapists who use the therapeutic system relying on manipulation of bones and muscles also use other Oriental medical techniques.

19   In most states of the U.S. Reiki and other alternative medicine practitioners can only provide their therapies for relaxation. You may want to seek information about the legal situation in your country with regard to this kind of alternative treatment.

20   In the old days people did not have a private bath at home, but went to a public bath-house with the whole family. This tradition still lives on and the art of bathing is one of the main relaxations in contemporary Japan.

21   Hayashi Sensei used to say that even Reiki could not help in such cases as the terminal stage of tuberculosis, syphilis and Hansen's disease.

22   In the time of Hayashi Sensei the names *Shoden* and *Okuden* were exchanged for other, more modern, Japanese names. *Shoden* became *Zenki* and *Okude* became *Kouki*. Originally 'Zenki' (first term) and 'Kouki' (latter term) were the names in the *Usui Reiki Ryoho Gakkai* for the two parts of the *Okuden* course. Hayashi Sensei taught in Tokyo and Osaka following the system of the *Gakkai* and taught *Shoden* and *Okuden* separately. But when he travelled to distant places such as Ishikawa, he taught only *Okuden*. However the content of that seminar included that of *Shoden* too, so actually the name was *Okuden* but he did not change the content of the seminar. In *Jikiden Reiki* I follow what Hayashi Sensei did in Ishikawa. I now use the name *Zenki* or *Shoden* and *Kouki* or *Okuden* to clarify the two levels. The words *Shoden* and *Okuden* have a much more traditional ring to them.

23   Sitting on one's knees Japanese style.

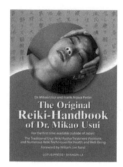

Dr. Mikao Usui and Frank A. Petter

The Original Reiki
Handbook of Dr. Mikao Usui

The Traditional Usui Reiki Ryoho Treatment Positions and
Numerous Reiki Techniques for Health and Well-Being

For the first time available outside of Japan: the original
hand positions from Dr. Usui's handbook. These treatment positions for a great variety of health complaints
have been listed in detail, making this work a valuable
reference guide for anyone who practices Reiki. Now, that
the original handbook has been translated into English,
Dr. Usui's hand positions and healing techniques can
be studied directly for the first time. Whether you are
an initiate or a Master, if you practice Reiki you can
expand your knowledge dramatically by following in
the footsteps of a great healer. Lavishly illustrated with
100 colored photos.

80 pages · 100 photographs · $14.95
ISBN 13: 978-0-914955-57-3
ISBN 10: 0-914955-57-8

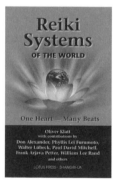

Oliver Klatt

Reiki Systems of the World

One Heart · Many Beats

With contributions by the leading Reiki Masters of
the world: Phyllis Lei Furumoto, Don Alexander, Walter
Lübeck, William Lee Rand, Paul David Mitchell, Frank Arjava
Petter

An inspiring and fascinating reference guide offering an
overview of the development of the world's Reiki systems.
For the first time anywhere, you obtain fundamental
information about internationally known and recognized
Reiki schools and lineages. You can also understand their
similarities and especially their differences on the basis
of practical examples and exercises. The author's warm-
hearted and sincere style is supported by his respect for,
and great knowledge of Reiki.

with 51 black&white drawings · 352 pages · $19.95
ISBN 13: 978-0-914955-79-5
ISBN 10: 0-914955-79-9

Frank Arjava Petter · Tadao Yamaguchi · Chujiro Hayashi

The Hayashi Reiki Manual

Traditional Japanese Healing Techniques from the Founder of the Western Reiki System

Dr. Chujiro Hayashi is the highly renowned student of Reiki founder, Dr. Mikao Usui. Dr. Hayashi developed his own style of Reiki and became the teacher of Hawayo Takata, who introduced Reiki to the West. However, Dr. Hayashi also taught Reiki to Japanese students such as young Chiyoko Yamaguchi, born in 1920. Frank Arjava Petter was allowed to become her student and learn the original Hayashi Reiki system from her. The manual presents the story of Dr. Hayashi, newly researched and sensationally illustrated with previously unpublished archive photos, Reiki techniques never taught in the West before, and specific documents such as the original certificates of Dr. Hayashi.

full color · 112 pages · $19.95
ISBN 13: 978-0-914955-75-7
ISBN 10: 0-914955-75-6

Walter Lübeck · Frank Arjava Petter

Reiki – Best Practices

Wonderful Tools of Healing for the First, Second and Third Degree of Reiki

Western Reiki techniques—published and presented in great detail for the first time

The internationally renowned Reiki Masters Walter Lübeck and Frank Arjava Petter introduce primarily Western Reiki techniques and place a valuable tool in the hands of every Reiki practitioner for applying Reiki in a specific and effective way for protection and healing.

A total of 60 techniques, such as: aura massage with Reiki, deprogramming of old patterns, karma clearing, protecting against energy loss, Tantra with Reiki are exclusively presented and described in detail for the first time in this fascinating guide.

296 pages · $19.95
ISBN 13: 978-0-914955-74-0
ISBN 10: 0-914955-74-8